How
I Got to Be
Whoever It Is
I Am

How
I Got to Be
Whoever
It Is I Am

Charles Grodin

SPRINGBOARD PRESS

NEW YORK   BOSTON

Grateful acknowledgment is given to Carson Entertainment for permission to reproduce letters sent to Charles Grodin by Johnny Carson.

Springboard Press
Hachette Book Group
237 Park Avenue, New York, NY 10017

Visit our Web site at www.HachetteBookGroup.com.

Springboard Press is an imprint of Grand Central Publishing. The Springboard name and logo are trademarks of Hachette Book Group, Inc.
Book design by Fearn Cutler de Vicq
Printed in the United States of America

First Edition: April 2009
10 9 8 7 6 5 4 3 2 1

Library of Congress Cataloging-in-Publication Data
Grodin, Charles.
    How I got to be whoever it is I am / Charles Grodin — 1st ed.
        p. cm.
    ISBN 978-0-446-51940-3
    1. Grodin, Charles. 2. Actors—United States—Biography. I. Title.
PN2287.G74A3 2009
792.02'8092—dc22
    [B]
                            2008040716

To all of us who are finding life a lot harder
than we had in mind

Author's Note

This book is the result of an effort to write about the events that informed my actions and values. It covers the 1940s to the present. I figure if I try to understand myself better, it may help me better understand others. Well . . . maybe not, but it can't hurt.

Contents

Contents

Contents

Contents

How
I Got to Be
Whoever It Is
I Am

Growing Up
in Pittsburgh, PA

My first memory of something having a powerful, lasting effect on me came when the Japanese
bombed Pearl Harbor on December 7, 1941.

I was a six-year-old growing up in Pittsburgh. I asked my
brother, Jack, who was twelve, if the Japanese would be coming
to Pittsburgh. He said, "Yes, they will." I asked, "Well . . . they
won't be coming to our house, will they?" He said, "Yes,
they will." I said, "Well . . . I'm going down to the basement.
They won't come down there, will they?" He said, "Yes,
they will."

Amazingly, that's the only tense moment I've ever had
with my brother. Decades later, he *did* once give me a look
when I commented on his orange golf pants.

I met my lifelong friend Herb Caplan when we were
four years old. We had moved into a small house with a
wall connecting to another small house, which had a wall
connecting to another small house. Herb and I shared a
wall. When we were around ten, we would pound on it to
get the other's attention and yell through it, mostly saying, "I'll meet you outside in five minutes." Amazingly,

our parents didn't complain, or more likely they weren't home.

Herb always has been and remains today one of my closest friends and one of the wisest. On my birthday, he said, "It's only a number," and if you read the obituaries you easily see what matters is not the number of your years but the state of your health. Recently, he said to a mutual friend who was complaining about this ache or that pain, "You can *make* yourself old." In other words, we can choose different ways to see things. Choose happy or at least positive thoughts. That may seem obvious, but how many of us do that?

Herb and I have had a lot of laughs over the years, but the best one he gave me recently. It's a true story.

When Herb's father, Larry Caplan, was in his eighties, Herb would accompany him into the doctor's examining room. The doctor once asked his dad, "Mr. Caplan, are you afraid of death?" Mr. Caplan said, "No, but I'd like to know *where* I'm going to die." When the doctor asked why that was important, Mr. Caplan said, "Then I won't *go* there."

My sixth through tenth years coincided with World War II. The headlines in the papers (there was no television then) were all about the Allied forces and the Axis forces. I knew the Allied forces were us and Great Britain and some other countries, and the Axis forces, the bad guys, were Germany, Japan, and Italy.

Although it wasn't really true, I somehow thought our Allied forces were doing great from the beginning. I had no doubt about the outcome. My inherent optimism that has served me so well through life showed itself very early.

In the years since the war, I've only encountered the Japanese in Japanese restaurants. They're always extraordinarily nice, although I get a little nervous when they do their hibachi thing and start flipping those knives around, but I would be nervous if *anyone* started flipping a knife around.

In the forties, the president was always President Roosevelt, the heavyweight champion of the world was Joe Louis, and the New York Yankees were the baseball champions. Those were the constants.

One day in 1945, when I was ten, I was walking home from Hebrew school and heard a radio on someone's porch on Mellon Street where my father's parents lived (as did Gene Kelly's family). A voice on the radio said that President Roosevelt had died. It was my first visceral experience that there were no constants. Everything has an expiration date.

Around the same time, a young friend of mine, Jerome Wesoky, was roller-skating down a hill at the corner of my street and hit a streetcar that had stopped to pick up passengers. He went under it. The conductor, not knowing, started up and the trolley went over Jerome, killing him.

Mr. Schwartz, who ran the grocery store at the corner, stood between the crane lifting the streetcar off Jerome and us kids who went to see what was going on. Thankfully, he made us turn our backs. Again I learned there are no constants. At ten, that was abundantly clear.

Oddly enough, or maybe not so oddly, right around that time I was impeached as president by the teacher of my fifth-grade class. She said it was because I talked incessantly. I find that hard to believe, but that's what she said, so it's probably true. I mean, why would someone make that up about a ten-year-old president? Besides, I'm perfectly capable of talking incessantly now, so I'm not a good witness for myself.

That was the first time I was removed, fired, kicked out—whatever you want to call it. Not that much later I got kicked out of Hebrew school for asking, I have to assume too many times, what the Hebrew words we were being asked to read on the blackboard meant. I honestly can't imagine I was rude, but looking back, I'd say my persistence in asking was considered rude by the rabbi. I always saw persistence simply as persistence, especially if it's done with respect, which I promise you is always how I persist. At least, that's *my* perception.

Getting kicked out of Hebrew school turned out to be a most fortunate experience, as it resulted in me studying with the father of my best friend, Raymond Kaplan. Rabbi Morris Kaplan was the only teacher I encountered in grammar school, high school, college, or acting class of whom I can say, "Now, that's a teacher!" At least, the only one I'd give an A.

Rabbi Kaplan wove spellbinding tales from the Old Testament. I remember walking down the street alone with him when I was about eleven. It was 1946. I asked him if we can dream when we die. He said, kindly, "No, sonny boy." That hit hard.

Years later, when I visited him in Los Angeles where he had become the head of the league of rabbis, I told him I had married a gentile girl. He put his head in his hands and sobbed. When he regained his composure, he said, "Children of parents who are Jewish and another religion become the biggest anti-Semites."

My daughter, Marion, considers herself Jewish even though the tradition is that a child takes the mother's religion. Marion also has as big a heart as anyone I've ever known. If a loved one is dying, I can't handle being there, which I see as a major flaw. I come only if asked. Marion, without being asked, crawls into bed beside the person.

So I had been impeached as president at ten and kicked out of Hebrew school at eleven. By the time I reached high school and our economics teacher, Mr. Kennedy, kicked me out of class, I was used to being kicked out. Again, it was for the same rap, asking too many questions or the same question too many times. I got high grades, and I always assumed that if I didn't understand something, some of the other kids wouldn't, either, but wouldn't say anything, so I jumped into the breach and was again kicked out. I learned early on that if there was a breach that needed jumping into and no one jumped, I would.

Unbeknownst to me, of course, all this being kicked out at a young age actually had a highly beneficial effect, because by the time I got into show business and was kicked out—fired— or threatened to be kicked out, I was used to it, so it lessened the blow. As time went by, without realizing it, I was developing a thick skin regarding criticisms I didn't agree with, so I was able to handle rejection, from what I've observed, better than most, who are often overwhelmed by it.

My Grandparents
and Other Loved Ones

A joyous part of my life in the 1940s was summertime in Chicago, where my grandparents, my cousins, and my aunt Ethel and uncle Bob lived.

I had occasion to speak of my grandfather, who was a Talmudic scholar, many years later when Ellis Island opened its new computer center. One of the other speakers was Irving Berlin's granddaughter. She said when her grandfather came to this country he was so impressed he wrote "Blue Skies." Joel Grey then got up and, accompanied by a piano player, sang "Blue Skies."

When my turn came to speak, I said, "When my grandfather came here, he wrote 'Green Skies,' but it never really clicked with the public." The audience laughed, but my son told me the man behind him sneeringly said, "This guy— *always* with the jokes!"

Spending over a decade of summers as a kid with my grandparents, aunt and uncle, and cousins was a treat. My bumpy moments with them came years later. Once my aunt Ethel looked up at me and really started to bawl me out about something. Oddly, I was amused, because I couldn't figure out what it was about. My cousin Fred recently told me my aunt was confronting me because of a hard time I had given some television host she liked. If that's true, my aunt would be one of the millions who didn't know I was joking with the hosts. At least the hosts knew.

My cousin Fred also told me recently that my grandfather was widely admired. "Congregants would come from all over to hear his witty interpretation of the Talmud." I was particularly struck by that when my wife read me something from a journal she had kept when our son, Nick, was growing up.

We had a Brazilian nanny who would come to Connecticut from New York on the train during the week to help look after our boy, who was then three. Nick listened as Regina told my wife that a man on the train had given her his card and asked her to go out with him. She showed the card to my wife, and my wife told her that Merrill Lynch was a financial organization, and according to the card this man was the head of one of its divisions, but Regina declined to go out with him, because, as she put it, "I don't know him or his family." Nick at three, listening to all this, asked, "So you're not going to go out with him?" Regina said, "I don't know him, so I can't." Nick persisted. "So you're not going to have dinner with him?" Regina again said, "No, I really don't know him, so I can't." Nick then said, "It's all right. He's my banker." Oh, if life worked differently, would my grandfather have enjoyed Nick!

My grandfather worked with me on my Bar Mitzvah, which took place in Chicago. He was then an old man with a long white beard. I will never forget him looking up at me from his chair and saying in appreciation, with a heavy accent, "a nomber von."

My only other memory of my grandfather talking to me was when he sat on the edge of my brother's bed in the bedroom we shared trying to convey to me that I should work harder to please my father. He pointed to his head and said in a deep, guttural voice, "Your father—his head is mmmmmmm," as if to say my father already had more than enough on his mind without having to deal with any problems with me.

As I recall, his crucially important words went right by me because I was so struck by the sight of this elderly Talmudic scholar with the big black hat and long white beard sitting on my brother's bed.

Even though my father and my uncle Bob gave them money, my grandparents had to take in boarders to help meet the bills. For a small fee, my grandmother would wash the boarders' clothes in the bathtub with a scrub board. Clotheslines were stretched across the back porch.

The boarders were not allowed to prepare food in my grandmother's kitchen. She was, of course, strictly kosher, as was my mother. I never understood the purpose of keeping a kosher kitchen, yet I who never stopped asking questions never asked why we separated meat from dairy. I'm sure it was explained to me at one point, but I forget, because I never had any interest in ritual. I'm only interested in character and behavior.

My grandmother Jennie Singer, along with her daughter, my mother, were my angels of goodness in childhood.

My female role model was my cousin Phyllis, who was warm and friendly and quick to laugh. When she was dying of cancer, I was going to fly down to Florida to spend some time with her. When she said, "My stomach is filled with cancer," she amazingly expressed no self-pity. She said to me, "Everyone wants to see you, but I'd rather see you alone." Before that opportunity presented itself, sadly, she died. When Phyllis had had her first child she named him Ted, after my dad, maybe because my dad helped support Phyllis and her younger brother, Fred, after their mother died and their father abandoned them.

This one ranks with my favorite memories of Chicago. When Phyllis's son Ted was about five years old, he spotted my great-uncle, Chiel Flassterstien, who he thought was his recently deceased great-grandfather, or Zadie as we called him. Ted said, "Zadie! I thought you died!" Without missing a beat, my great-uncle Chiel responded, "I came back."

In my early twenties I went to my cousin Fred's wedding in Chicago. My grandmother was in the hospital. I went to see her. She was her usual cheerful self with me. From my earliest sight of her she filled my heart with love that never wavered. I don't remember her ever looking at me without a smile on her face. After our visit I kissed her and left. Halfway down the hall, I remembered something I forgot to tell her. I turned around to go back to her room , but when I got to the door, I didn't go in, because of what I saw. Jennie Singer didn't see me, because she was convulsed with sobs. She knew she had just said goodbye forever to her grandson.

From Thirteen
to Eighteen Years Old

I was very fortunate to grow up in a household of role models. My father, mother, and brother all worked hard, and I don't remember any nasty comments about other people ever expressed in our house. That doesn't mean they loved everyone, but they were never nasty or hostile. I'm sure that's why today I'm good at cutting slack for others, as I hope they'll do for me.

When I was in eighth grade in 1948, I was the seventh man on my grammar school basketball team. I loved playing basketball. As years went by, I was in a league at the Y with some of my teammates from grammar school. A fellow named Bill Goren who worked at the Y and was a friend of my family observed me playing. He called me into his office one day and said, "The other boys seem to be developing their skills more than you." I said, "I know." He asked, "Why is that?" I said, "I don't know."

I thought about it in later years and came to the conclusion that basketball for me was always just fun. If you really wanted to excel, you had to go full out to *beat* the other guy, something I really wasn't interested in doing.

About twenty years later when I was in a pickup basketball game with other men, playing in my usual have-fun style, I remembered the conclusion I'd come to about excelling at basketball. In the middle of the game I thought to myself, *If all you need to do is really put out much more effort to excel, why don't you do it right now and find out if you're kidding yourself?* Though it might sound self-serving, I have to say that the minute I went full out, I dominated the game. In competitive sports, if you're not ready to give everything you have every moment, don't even bother showing up. Of course, that largely applies to life itself.

When I was a kid we had radio and movies. Movies were like a magic world, but radio was right there in our house, a member of the family. I think that's why being on the radio these past several years has meant more to me than being in the movies or on television.

I remember a big red portable radio I often used to take to bed and put under the covers. Since my brother was six years older and usually went to bed later, I could listen to it until he came to bed and said nicely, "Could you turn your radio off?"

Looking back, I think I formed a lot of my values from the radio. I found a lot of heroes there—Superman, Batman, but mostly the Lone Ranger. There was something about the way he would ride off before anyone had a chance to thank him, and there'd always be one person who'd say, "Who was that masked man?" I got a particular thrill when the answer would come, "Why, that was the Lone Ranger!"

Several years ago there was quite a to-do in the news about the Lone Ranger. Some Hollywood producers were planning a new movie about him and were searching for someone to play him. During my childhood, the Lone Ranger was played by Brace Beemer on the radio. When the Lone Ranger moved to television, I was among the legions of fans who continued to follow him.

For us, there was only one Lone Ranger on television, and his name was Clayton Moore. Even as we grew older, he was still there. But now Hollywood wanted to make a big movie of the Lone Ranger, and Clayton Moore was seventy. Oh, he was still around. In fact, he was still around as the Lone Ranger. Nobody had seen him leap up on many horses lately, but he was still showing up at parades and rodeos, and getting plenty of cheers and applause, too.

But Hollywood was making a big new Lone Ranger movie, and the search was on for the new, young Lone Ranger. The producers of the movie felt it would not be in their interest to have two Lone Rangers around, so they went to court to get a ruling to force Clayton Moore to take off his mask and stop appearing as the Lone Ranger, and they won. *Our* Lone Ranger was ordered to take off his mask.

Clayton Moore had worn his mask his whole life. Without it, well, he just wasn't the Lone Ranger. If you've been the Lone Ranger your whole life, it's kind of tough, at seventy, to take off your mask and stop being him. So Clayton Moore went to court and protested the ruling, but he lost. Our Lone Ranger had to take off his mask.

Years earlier there was a headline in a New York newspaper. It read: SUPERMAN COMMITS SUICIDE. George Reeves, who had been Superman about as long as Clayton Moore had been the Lone Ranger, had committed suicide, having become despondent over being unable to find work as an actor after the *Superman* television series was canceled. Whenever he would try to get a part in something, they would say, "We can't use you in that part. People will say, 'That's Superman!'" And so he couldn't get a job, got very depressed, and ended his life.

Our Lone Ranger, Clayton Moore, fought back. When the court ordered him to take off his mask, he appealed the decision to a higher court. The next time anyone saw him in public, he had taken off the mask pending appeal, but in its place was a very large pair of dark sunglasses, not a bad mask in its own right. He showed up with those big dark sunglasses that covered just as much of his face as the mask had, and the applause and cheers were louder than ever. The public was on his side.

Meanwhile, the Hollywood producers found a young man named Klinton Spilsbury to be the new Lone Ranger. The movie was made. It came out, and nobody went to see it. There were at least a couple of reasons for this. It hadn't gotten good reviews, and also, by the time it came out, there was quite a lot of public resentment over taking the mask off *our* Lone Ranger.

Eventually, a higher court ruled that Clayton Moore could wear the mask, after all. The glasses came off, the mask went back on, and Clayton Moore was getting bigger cheers than ever before!

Shortly after this I was at a party and got into a conversation with a young actor who turned out to be Klinton

Spilsbury, the new movie's Lone Ranger. He told me that he was a serious actor from New York, had studied a lot, and was really doing very well moving up the ladder when this Lone Ranger opportunity came along. He said the movie was a mess. There were several scripts, and no one could agree on whether they were supposed to be funny or serious. He was having difficulty finding work because of his association with the movie and had moved back to New York to try to pick up the pieces of his career, which basically had ended. The movie had a devastating effect on everyone except Clayton Moore, who was more popular than ever.

When I was a kid, we had a saying, "Don't mess with the Lone Ranger."

As the story went, when a troop of rangers were killed by the Indians, only one ranger survived, and he was nursed back to health by an Indian, Tonto. When the ranger first regained consciousness he asked the Indian, "What happened?" Tonto said, "All rangers killed. You Lone Ranger." I got goose bumps.

Who among us has not sometimes felt like the lone ranger? Not the Lone Ranger, but the *lone* ranger?

High School

I entered Peabody High School in 1949. Eighth-grade graduates from various grammar schools came to Peabody, where the kids were then put in 9B, then 9A, 10B, 10A, 11B, 11A, 12B, 12A. We were divided into three different homerooms starting in 9B, so we were meeting a lot of new kids for the first time.

A few weeks into 9B, I was home in bed, sick with a cold. When my mother came into the bedroom I shared with my brother to tell me a classmate had called, I couldn't have known that something important had just happened. She told me that I'd been elected president of my freshman homeroom class, *and I hadn't even been there.* This was the beginning of a series of events that was to have a powerful effect on me for the rest of my life.

I went on to be elected president of my homeroom in 9A, then of 10B and 10A as a sophomore, of 11B and 11A as a junior, and of 12B as a senior. Next, all three 12A homerooms made me president. The margins grew wider at each election. All this happened to a boy who had been impeached as president in the fifth grade.

I couldn't have realized it at the time, but this gave me an unusually high level of confidence that has never wavered. Granted, I only aspire to what I believe I can achieve. I guarantee you I'll never be chosen scientist of the year.

When I was in my teens, my brother suggested that we form a law firm together. He was in law school and I was in high school, but something about me provoked my brother to say that. Not only did he want to partner with me, he wanted to be the research guy, and I would be the courtroom guy.

When my son, Nick, was graduated from middle school at thirteen, my wife and I listened as the principal said something about each kid as they crossed the stage to receive their certificate. "She really can spell," for example, or "He won the two-mile race." As Nick went up I leaned forward to hear what was going to be said, and I'll never forget the principal's words: "He really knows how to marshal an argument." If my brother had known Nick at the time Jack was in law school, he would have asked him to be the courtroom guy and the head of the firm.

Recently, I came across the yearbook of my graduating class. It listed the best and the most, in about twenty categories—most likely to succeed, funniest, smartest, etc. There was the best and the second best in all categories, with separate listings for boys and girls. My name didn't appear once. It took me back to a conversation I had with the only African American girl in my class, Joanne Snyder. I asked her why I kept getting elected. She said, "You care about people." It's interesting to me that there wasn't a caring category in "the best, the most" in high school then. I hope there is today, but I'm doubtful. I had no idea that was unique, and still find it hard to grasp. Today it resonates, because every time I agree to host a charity event, the organizers seem shocked to learn I won't take a fee. *I'm* shocked that that's unusual.

An odd thing happened when I was around seventeen. Miss Owen, the extremely pugnacious woman who was in charge of the school play, aggressively confronted me in the hall one day. She was angry that she didn't see my name on the list of people who were going to audition for the senior class play. I explained to her that I wasn't available because I had to work in my dad's store, but she wasn't buying. She just flat-out didn't believe me! I had never given a thought to acting.

My plan was to go to the University of Pittsburgh and major in journalism. I had been the humor editor of my grammar school paper and also worked on the high school paper.

Miss Owen absolutely believed that I wasn't auditioning because I didn't like her. I've never been big on disliking people unless they gave me a really good reason, and Miss Owen certainly hadn't. I didn't even dislike any of the people who kept kicking me out of things. Oh, maybe for a moment, but generally I can understand someone kicking me out, even if I don't agree. That remains true today.

What was really odd about that confrontation with Miss Owen was when I asked her why she was so vehement about my auditioning for the class play, since she had never seen me act. She said with great certainty, "I know you'd be good and you know it, too!"

My only theatrical experience had been playing the role

of Don in *Getting Gracie Graduated,* our eighth-grade class play. Miss McCallum gave me the part because (surprise, surprise), just like Don, I asked so many questions. Since I had no idea how to act, I only distinguished myself by learning all my lines and everyone else's, so I could whisper to them if they forgot, which is what happened. In any case, because of my obligation to work in my father's store, I never auditioned for the senior class play.

There's so much I don't understand about what we were asked to study in high school, and talking to high school kids today confirms for me that it's still largely the case. There were many courses that I and most others had no interest in at all. Latin, algebra, and geometry, not to mention the dreaded trigonometry, quickly come to mind. Let's throw in chemistry. In spite of my questioning nature, I generally went with the flow as far as the courses were concerned, because I felt I had no choice.

I don't understand why those courses were obligatory. They made most of us want to run out the back door screaming. I got high grades only because I have a retentive mind, not because I was interested—that, and they sometimes graded on the beloved curve, meaning other kids were close to having breakdowns.

About twenty years ago I asked an algebra teacher what the purpose of algebra was. She couldn't answer me. One friend who claims to know everything, including where we were before we were born and where we go after we die, said, "Algebra teaches logic." I love my friend, but I wouldn't say logic is his strong suit. The metaphysical? Maybe.

I'd be for developing a curriculum that includes teaching how to get through life the best you can. How to be a good partner, a good friend, a good daughter or son, a good parent, the importance of helping those in need, and so forth are subjects that quickly come to mind. Do we have people who could teach those courses? On the other hand, I didn't find the teachers of the courses I was told to take effective. They never explained why we were studying these things, and I who was never at a loss for questions must have been—in the science and math areas anyway—too numb to ask. Ironically, I once took an aptitude test that said I should be an accountant. In the future, I would *play* an accountant, but *be* one? Yeah, right.

I also didn't question my third-grade teacher's right to hit us across our knuckles for talking or how the shop teacher could whack seventh- and eighth-grade kids (not me) with a paddle for talking. I'd seen enough by high school, so when Mr. Myers, the gym teacher and basketball coach, grabbed me by the arm, I tore it away from him and gave him a look I'm sure surprised him. Early on it was clear to me that while I somehow managed to get along unusually well with others, I had a very strong reaction to anything I viewed as inappropriate.

Decades later, the producer Ray Stark was giving my girlfriend, who was directing a movie for him, a very hard time. I had more than one conversation with myself to stop myself from physically going after him. I succeeded—barely. Later, I attacked him in print. He, of course, retaliated in print, not using his name but through a columnist he had in his pocket. He got the columnist to take a cheap shot at me. What else is new?

Frankly, I don't think I've yet fully recovered from "single file, no talking" in grammar school. I mean, what was *that* all about?! As I remember, everyone changed classes at the same time, so we wouldn't be disturbing kids in class. I mean, this was Pittsburgh, in America—not a fascist country.

I was rushed by fraternities at the University of Pittsburgh. My only memory of that is sitting in a fraternity house with a group of guys watching porno movies. I was astonished and still am at the idea. As a kid, I remember driving around the park with buddies talking about "getting a feel" of this or that girl, meaning getting to touch a breast, never a bare one. When they finished talking of their exploits they looked at me to offer something, but I never did. This annoyed them. They said, "You're listening to us!" I told them I wasn't going to tell them what they should talk about, but I wasn't going to join in. Also, it's not as though I had anything to offer.

Later, I became a vocal critic of Howard Stern and Don Imus and always questioned what was permitted to be aired. I once asked Walter Cronkite, who said, "Community standards define that." I so admire Mr. Cronkite, but I'm still not sure what community he was referring to.

Howard Stern once said my son would probably grow up to be a fan of his. He couldn't have been more wrong. Howard Stern thought it was amusing on television to hold up some bones of a young woman who had been cremated and make jokes about them. *Standards?* What does it say about us that someone like that could have so many fans? To me, it says a significant percentage of us need to grow up! At least *seek* some maturity. More recently, the third most popular radio host in America, Michael Savage, attacked kids with autism by saying, "In ninety-nine percent of the cases, it's a brat who hasn't been told to cut the act out. That's what autism is." I'm a mentor to a teenager with a form of autism. I promise you, Michael Savage doesn't know what he's talking about. He's the one who should cut the act out. Sadly, hate sells.

Girls

My situation with girls in the 1940s and the early '50s wasn't good—to put it mildly. It started in eighth grade with a mad crush on Cookie Riedbord, but Cookie wouldn't go out with me because I was too short—at least four inches shorter than Cookie, who had a mad crush on the high school quarterback, Pete Neft. I was about five one then. Now I'm six feet, but this is now, and that was then. I moved on in high school to an even madder crush on Judy Gotterer. She was the star of the class play, a cheerleader, and the editor of the school paper, along with being gorgeous. Judy wouldn't go out with me because I was too young—six months younger than she was.

Recently, my daughter, who is a stand-up comedian, was appearing in Pittsburgh. Some of my friends from the Pittsburgh Playhouse showed up and told her that all the girls had a crush on me when I was there. I knew about one girl, but I had no idea about anyone else. Then I came across a high school graduation picture of a girl I'd known since kindergarten. On the back of her picture she wrote, "All the girls had a crush on you." I was oblivious to that as well. I've never assumed that if a girl or woman smiles and is friendly to me it means anything other than she's friendly to me. Oh, well . . .

One of my attitudes about sex and romance that caused me a lot of problems first occurred in high school. A beautiful girl transferred to our school from Tennessee; I asked her to the prom, and she accepted. She wasn't older or taller than I was. We began to date. I don't even remember kissing her.

One evening she felt she should tell me she had been married. She was only seventeen when I knew her. I took her to the prom, but in my Jewish-raised orthodox mind, all bets for anything serious like marriage were off.

The attitude of no sex before marriage, for girls anyway, was the dominant moral code of the fifties. This changed completely in the sixties. My big problem was that I couldn't make the change. I couldn't imagine marrying anyone who wasn't a virgin. As years went by, close to twenty-five years, anyway, this became a serious problem, because there didn't seem to be any virgins.

Sometime in the sixties when I was still in the throes of this "you have to be a virgin before marriage" issue, my girlfriend said to me, "Aren't you happy for me that I've had a lot of wonderful sexual experiences?" It was a rare instance when I was rendered speechless.

Later in the sixties, I went out with a girl who said she was a virgin, and I believed her. I actually considered marrying her, but I realized that although the woman I was going to marry should be a virgin, maybe a marriage should have

more going for it than a woman's virginity. Quite hypocriti-
cally, I didn't apply that rule to myself. I believe I saw the
light when someone asked me if I wanted my daughter to be
a virgin prior to marriage. Immediately, I said she should
do whatever makes her happy that doesn't land her in jail.
I couldn't have a double standard when it came to my own
kid, so that affected my attitude quite a bit. I believe it's a
good idea to try to personalize everyone's situation. It can't
help but raise your empathy level.

My attitude toward virginity really went away when I got
in touch with my mortality. It terms of being bothered by
something, mortality easily trumped lack of virginity.

Dad

I'm named after my father's father, so according to Jewish tradition he would have to have been deceased when I was born. I don't remember ever meeting my father's mother. Sometime in the nineteenth century a relative whose identity neither my brother nor I knows changed the name Grodinski to Grodin.

My father had a store where he sold supplies for cleaners, tailors, and dressmakers: materials for suits, linings, zippers, buttons, and hangers, for example. My interest in our nation's justice system began when I was fourteen. Now I'm preoccupied with it on a daily basis. A Negro boy, as African Americans were then called, who worked for my dad was arrested for something. He was out on bail, but my father kept him on. When I said, "But he's been arrested," my father replied, "He hasn't been convicted." Dad taught me the principle of innocent until proven guilty at an early age. I believe that my sense of fairness and the feeling that it was not right for me to be kicked out of things somehow joined forces at that time.

Since I had started kindergarten at four and Hebrew

school at seven, by the time I got to high school at fourteen I wanted to be free after school to be involved with sports.

My dad felt I was lazy because I couldn't bring myself to work in his store as much as my brother dutifully had. When I did show up, I remember sitting on a counter counting up grosses of buttons, among other mundane tasks, and wishing I could be somewhere else playing sports of *any* kind. While my confidence was growing with every passing election, unbeknownst to me something else was happening that was to have an equally powerful effect.

The tug-of-war between my dad and me over how much time I should spend in the store ended in a standoff. I was there, but not enough as far as Dad was concerned.

My father had been in and out of hospitals his whole life, but when he suddenly died at 4:55 p.m. on June 26, 1953, at the age of fifty-two, I was in complete shock. I was eighteen, and I know I haven't really recovered. Our relationship had so deteriorated, from his point of view, that he asked me to put all requests for anything in writing, even though we lived in a small six-room house. "Anything," in my case, meant getting to use the car, which Dad used to make deliveries.

It couldn't have helped my cause that when Dad let me have the car to take my driver's test, which I passed on the third try, I drove up to my dad's store, saw him standing in front, and shouted out the window, "Dad, I passed, I passed," and crashed into the car parked in front of me! However, he later said, "You're probably a better driver than I am, but I'm too nervous."

More than one person has suggested that my penchant

for being involved in so many charities has to do with my guilt over my relationship with my dad. If I know them well enough I point out what Joanne Snyder said before my dad's passing about my caring for others. Nevertheless, I obviously didn't have the insight to know I wasn't caring enough about my dad.

I still consider the way I dealt with my father my biggest mistake in life. It's the one I chose to write about for the book *If I Only Knew Then . . . Learning from Our Mistakes.* My lesson was that if you love someone, even if you think you're right, don't try to prevail if you will cause your loved one stress. I know that now. Regretfully I didn't know it as a teenager.

Dad did live to see me give the valedictorian address at my high school commencement. In my school, the valedictorian wasn't the person with the highest grades but the class president. There were probably some 4.0s among us. I was about a 3.7.

In any case, I know my dad was proud and, I'm sure, astonished to see me up there.

University of Miami

J ust before I was going to graduate from high school and go to the University of Pittsburgh, I saw a movie, *A Place in the Sun*. I fell in love with Elizabeth Taylor, and as I watched Montgomery Clift I marveled at how easy acting seemed. On the spot, again thinking I could do anything I aspired to, I decided to be an actor instead of a journalist. Of course, I had no idea what I was getting into. My mother said, "Nobody makes a living in that field." I didn't realize how close to the truth that was. I simply said, "I'll outwork everyone." I don't remember my dad hearing me say that. If Mother ever told him, I can only imagine the look of disbelief on his face.

I've always been fortunate to have a lot of friends, but sometime around my sophomore year in high school I developed a close friendship with another kid that was different from anything I had ever experienced.

We were about the same age, but he seemed older, more sophisticated. He was the one who had his own car—a red convertible. He was the one who was first to have sex with his girlfriend, something just about unheard of in high school in the fifties in Pittsburgh.

He was also devoted to me. When I kept getting elected president of the class, he identified with me so much, he said he felt *he* was getting elected. Some other buddies and I all looked up to him. He exuded confidence. Some of us even called him "Chief."

I went to the University of Miami in Florida because he suggested it. I don't know if Miami had a better drama department than the University of Pittsburgh. I never inquired about Carnegie Mellon (Carnegie Tech, as it was then called), even though it had the reputation of having one of the best drama departments in the country. It was in Pittsburgh, but I never even considered it. I can only assume that, having just lost my dad, I wanted to be around my best friend.

He graduated six months ahead of me and told me there was a dean from Pittsburgh at the University of Miami, and after a semester he felt I would be given a scholarship. I didn't even question how that would happen. I just applied, got in, and went in September 1953.

Even though I wasn't really aware of it, after my dad's passing everything changed. I should have realized things were different, because I began to mess up in ways I never had before. I had graduated in February and wasn't starting college for about six months, so I got a job at a local Buick dealership. I was a car jockey, which meant I was to drive new Buicks into different empty spaces in the huge showroom. I had never driven a car that went forward just by putting it in drive without touching the accelerator, so after denting a few new Buicks, I was told they wouldn't need me on Friday. This was on a Thursday, so I asked, "Should I come in on Monday?" The answer was a simple no. Looking back, it was a very kind firing. A while later I was fired from a Mary Jane shoe store in Miami because I couldn't find the shoes my female customer was wearing when she walked in! Talk about being preoccupied.

Ironically, my relationship with my friend began to unravel because I was no longer willing to look up to anyone. I guess I felt I had to take charge of everything in my life. I never looked down on anyone, but now I no longer looked up to anyone, either.

We were driving to the University of Miami in September. A third fella from another high school in Pittsburgh whom we had just met and who was to be a roommate was with us. My friend and I got into what began as a slight disagreement about, of all things, the color of the car in front of us. One of us felt it was dark green and the other black.

If we'd had disagreements in the past, and frankly I don't remember any, I would concede the point, because, after all, he was the chief, but this time I didn't. The dynamic of the friendship shifted right there over a meaningless disagreement about the color of a car. We drove the rest of the way to Florida pretty much in silence. The other kid looked on, I'm sure, baffled.

The three of us moved into an off-campus apartment. The other guy and I became buddies, and my former closest friend and I barely spoke. Quite simply, I no longer saw him as in charge, and we had lost what he must have seen as that essential condition.

I now know I was in a depression after my dad died, but I didn't realize it then. I should have found it unusual that I, who had always been a happy kid, was suddenly staring into space for long periods of time. Worse, on more than one occasion I remember swimming far out in the Atlantic Ocean alone, with no one around. Unconsciously, I was being self-destructive. I mean, that's where the sharks are.

I had one date at this so-called playboy school, the University of Miami, and I still had yet to kiss a girl, at least as far as I remember. Because of my depression, I had no interest in anything, including girls. Ellen Burstyn writes in her memoir that the first time I kissed her onstage in *Same Time, Next Year* . . . well, let's just say she found it memorable. I had no idea I had so much to offer.

Three things happened at the university that were good signs for my future show-business endeavors.

All incoming freshman were given information about the university—kind of an orientation test. There was no grade, but they did announce that out of around a thousand students, only one got a perfect score. Young Chuck Grodin was now working hard at everything, and that's obviously essential if you want to be successful, whatever your job.

I was taking a course in semantics. At one point the teacher announced that someone from the class would be asked to get up in front of a large assembly and give a speech. He said we would be given plenty of notice. One day, without any warning, he announced that we were going to a hall filled with hundreds of students, and one of us would volunteer to give a speech. The class nervously went into the assembly hall. No one wanted to get up there, so I did, following my pattern of jumping in if no one else did.

In front of at least five hundred people, I told a story about going on a hunting trip in Pennsylvania with my girlfriend. When the girl and I drifted in different directions, I went looking for her. In the distance I saw a bear dragging her lifeless body into the woods. I chased the bear, but never found it or my girlfriend.

Nobody said the story had to be true, but from that time on, I would often be pointed out on campus as the kid who lost his girlfriend to a bear. Looking back on my six months at the University of Miami, I realize I never factored in until recently that my unusual ability at eighteen to tell a story in front of five hundred people was definitely a good sign.

I had gone to the university to be a drama major so was very surprised to learn that, as an incoming freshman, I was not allowed to take an acting class. Somehow, I suppose because of the craziness of that concept, I was able to persuade an administrator to allow me into one. I've found common sense often will prevail.

Fortunately the class was taught by the head of the department, Professor Howard Koch. I remember going onstage only once. I did a monologue from *Julius Caesar*. On the way to the class I was so nervous I wished the ground would open up and swallow me. After all, my only other time on a stage was in *Getting Gracie Graduated* in eighth grade.

I couldn't really understand *Julius Caesar*, but I was able to connect with the monologue, which I thought was about injustice. Later I realized it was a lot more complicated than that, but happily I didn't know it at the time. At eighteen, I could identify with injustice, and as I began to shout out "Friends, Romans, countrymen, lend me your ears," it seemed my body stopped shaking to hear what I had to say.

As my inspirational actor Montgomery Clift once said, "The body doesn't know you're acting." After I was finished, a very pretty girl in the first row stared at me with a look I had never seen on a girl's face, at least on a girl's face looking at *me*. More importantly, Professor Koch said to me, "If you work hard, there's no limit to how far you can go."

I didn't know at the time that those would be the last words of real encouragement I would hear for years from someone in authority.

At the Christmas break, I went home and auditioned for a scholarship at the Pittsburgh Playhouse. The monologue from *Julius Caesar* got me one. When I was in Pittsburgh during the break I suddenly realized there were no African Americans at the University of Miami. Racism was so taken for granted as the American way of life then. Unfortunately, I believe it still overwhelmingly is.

Only recently has it occurred to me that my place so soon after my father's passing should have been with my mother. My brother had married, and my mom was alone. I'm stunned and embarrassed that I never thought of that.

I left Miami after six months and went to the Playhouse. I had no contact with my former friend, who remained in Florida and went into business there. Almost twenty years later, I was in Miami promoting a movie I had done, and I looked him up. We got together, and the evening was cordial, but that was it.

He came to see me a few years later in a Broadway show with my name on the marquee. He came to my dressing room afterward, sat on a sofa, and suddenly began to sob. I had no idea why. Eventually, he said, "No one could imagine you would be so successful, but I did." I would be guessing as to why that provoked this man of forty to sob, and your guess would be as good as mine. In any case, after that night we never saw or spoke to each other again. Many relationships of all kinds just can't survive a change in the dynamic.

The Military

In 1953, I enlisted in the Naval Reserve in Pittsburgh. We weren't at war, but we still had a draft, and I assumed at some point I would be drafted by the Army, and I would lose two years of pursuing my profession.

The enlistment was for eight years and required me to go to meetings once a week, go to boot camp, and be out at sea two weeks a year. I started reporting to the weekly meetings. My main memory is how much the uniform itched, and how hard it was for me to concentrate on how torpedoes work.

There was something very wrong with my enlistment, although it wasn't until years later that I realized it. Someone at the recruiting office should have told me that this was not a good idea for me because I couldn't possibly go to weekly meetings, since I knew I'd be traveling to pursue the acting profession.

Eventually, I got a letter notifying me I was now in the active status pool. I had no idea what that meant and didn't even ask. I was extremely naïve. When I was around twenty-three, I received my draft notice from the Army. I reported and passed the physical. While I was waiting for the actual notice to be inducted, I realized I could still join a reserve unit, so I began to call around, but there were no openings. Then I called the Naval Reserve. They had no openings, either. I said, "I used to be with you people." There was a silence at the other end of the phone. Finally, the man said, "Were you discharged?" I said, "No." He said, "Then you're still in the Naval Reserve."

It had been around five years since I joined, so I had three more years of meetings, and then I'd be discharged. Up until then I might have gone to a meeting once a week for a couple of months. But when I was settled in New York, I went to the Brooklyn Navy Yard, joined a reserve unit, and reported every week for three years. It was only then that I came to understand that being in the active status pool meant that if there was a call-up of troops, I'd be on the front lines. I was playing Russian roulette without knowing it.

I went to boot camp where a drill instructor found it necessary to scream obscenities at us. Every year I would be out at sea for two weeks on a large warship, often off the coast of North Carolina, at Cape Hatteras.

I progressed from seaman recruit to seaman apprentice to seaman to quartermaster third class, which is another name for navigator. That's really ironic, since I have an unusually poor sense of direction.

One extremely foggy night at sea, they assigned me the forward watch. From four a.m. to eight a.m., I was to stand at the very front of the ship for a possible visual sighting of another ship, which I guess our radar could miss. Having a very active imagination, within five minutes I spotted more than one large ship heading our way and alerted the bridge. Our large warship came to an abrupt stop and began to reverse engines. Soon they realized there was nothing out there and told me to go back to bed.

Once I picked up a microphone that allowed me to speak to the entire ship. There was a Jerry Lewis–type kid who was kind of my sidekick. I said on the ship's PA system, "Foreman, that is Foreman, report to the top deck, on the double! That is *Foreman!*" The poor kid raced up to the top deck and arrived in a minute out of breath to see me standing there smiling at him. I still can't believe I actually did that.

I enjoyed my three years in the Naval Reserve. The best moment was when an African American sailor and I listened on the radio to Floyd Patterson regaining his heavyweight championship by knocking out Ingmar Johansson. We leapt in the air and hugged each other.

The lesson of my enlistment as a teenager is that the military has to fully divulge what the deal is. Obviously, it wasn't explained to me what would happen if I didn't show up. Of course, this *really* becomes important during times of war when recruiters put such a stress on bonuses and opportunities and rarely mention possible death.

I know to this day wildly inappropriate things are going on in the military. There are stories about the Army asking some veterans for part of their enlistment bonus back. To get out of paying benefits, they sometimes claim psychological problems are caused by "prior personality disorder." That's not official policy, but it has been happening. The head of a veterans' organization in Washington told me there are some twenty-five thousand cases of this. President Bush signed a bill to look into it.

There are also at this writing two hundred thousand homeless veterans in America. Support the troops? What exactly does that mean?

Many years later, I was on Larry King's television show. He asked me if I had been in the military. I openly dodged the question. He waited a moment and asked me again. I openly ducked the question once more. Eventually, he asked again. This time I said, "I was in the Naval Reserve." He then asked, "Why were you so reluctant to answer the question?" I said "Well . . . I wasn't on our side."

The Pittsburgh Playhouse

At the Pittsburgh Playhouse I first ran into the abuse common to so many acting classes, which are overwhelmingly taught by people who couldn't make a living as actors. First at the Playhouse and later in New York, I was doing something that no one else was doing—no longer a surprise—asking questions.

At the Playhouse, I was asking about the "Method" that was new to American actors. Since no one there had any knowledge of it, the head of the school made fun of me for trying to "live the part." He and his protégé were once making what I'm sure they felt was good-natured fun of me: "Look at him. Look at him trying to live the part."

Of course, I was too inexperienced to achieve it, but I knew inhabiting the character was the goal. I answered them, with a confidence I actually had, "I'll be famous someday, and you guys will be out of the business." Even though I hardly ever speak so arrogantly, I learned early on that when I'm confronted inappropriately, I get rougher than the person who confronts me.

I actually can't remember one thing that was taught

about acting at the Playhouse. I do remember a teacher who for reasons known only to him chose to unzip his fly and zip it up again while teaching.

The big value there—and it *was* a big value—was the ongoing opportunity to get up in front of people and do scenes. Obviously, no matter what you aspire to, you've got to *do* it, and I spent a year and a half there acting in front of people. I hadn't had the opportunity to do that, with the exception of *Getting Gracie Graduated* in eighth grade and the monologue from *Julius Caesar* at the University of Miami.

A nationally known speech teacher came over from Carnegie Tech to teach. She had us all striving for what she called mid-Atlantic speech, and what I called an English accent. I would say five sentences and she had pages of notes criticizing how I spoke. I remember thinking Montgomery Clift and Spencer Tracy didn't have English accents but sounded like Americans, so I didn't give a moment's thought to all those absurd speech notes. Plenty of actors followed her advice, but I'm not aware of any you or I have ever heard of. There's not a huge demand for actors who sound English in America, and if there ever is, they'll get them from England.

My high point at the Playhouse came when I was in a student production of *Charley's Aunt.* I played Sir Francis Chesney. In order to get to where I entered I had to crawl behind the set and beneath a window from left stage. I entered and brought the house down with everything I said and did. I thought, "Oh, my God, what a response! Maybe they'll name a theater after me someday." When I came offstage everyone was laughing, because there was whipped cream all over the tails of my full-dress coat. I'd picked it up from the floor behind the window where I had crawled. The audience was laughing, but I was thinking, "Maybe not *all* the laughs came from the whipped cream." Always the optimist!

It was a revelation for me first at the Playhouse, then in Uta Hagen's class and in Lee Strasberg's class, that there were plenty of gifted people. I saw as many as a hundred over a ten-year period who were as good or better than actors or actresses you see in the movies or on Broadway, but I can count on one hand those who became known. There were too many aspirants for too few opportunities. Also, very few could handle the endless rejection.

Recently, I read a ridiculous rationale for the cruelty expressed on the television show *American Idol.* Someone said words to the effect that if you were going into show business, you better get used to cruelty. Rejection? Yes. But there is never any justification for cruelty, and almost always it comes around to bite the person who thinks there is.

The Pittsburgh Playhouse was also an eye-opener for me regarding sex. I had never run into gay men, so I had no idea how many of the staff and students were gay. Since I've always had a lot of male friends, I began to make friends with some of the staff and a local actor who sometimes appeared in the main stage productions.

Once this actor and I were driving around the park, as I always did with my high school buddies. We parked by the reservoir and talked. At one point I said, "Let's take a walk around the reservoir." He said, "Someone might see us." I had no idea what he was talking about. I said, "Someone might see us? What'ya mean?" He said, "You *are* gay, aren't you?" I said, "Me? No, I'm not gay." It was very uncomfortable in the car as I drove him home. Another gay fellow told me that I just hadn't met the right man yet. I still haven't.

I took a walk in the park with another guy who worked at the Playhouse. I didn't think he was gay until he suggested we sit on the grass on our jackets. I said I didn't want to sit on my jacket. He said he didn't care about his jacket, so he put it down for me to sit on. I tried to quickly think of a way to get out of there with a minimum amount of embarrassment. When he ran his fingers through my hair, I leapt up and took off over a hill. So much for a minimum of embarrassment.

I should say that on those rare occasions in my life when a woman has come on to me, I don't run over a hill, but I do withdraw. Since I don't like that and I've never been aggressive toward a woman, it's hard even for *me* to imagine how I ever had dates.

Not long ago my wife and I went to a black-tie event given by a famous female television personality. At some point in the evening, she approached me from the side. I didn't see her coming. She planted a big smacker on my lips! My wife was standing right beside me, but even if she hadn't been, I wouldn't have appreciated it.

Of course, since so many of the guys at the Playhouse were gay, I had almost no competition, if any, for the girls. I had my first sexual romance with a dazzling girl there. She was the young musical comedy star, not of the school but of the whole theater, and she was a teenager. She later made it to Broadway and the movies. The last time I saw her, about forty years ago, she had suffered some kind of a brain tumor and gained a lot of weight. She asked me if I would hang out with her for an afternoon and take a look at about ten dresses she had put a hold on.

When I thought of that beautiful young girl and compared her to the heavyset woman I was now talking to who was obviously having some mental difficulties, it was a jarring reminder of what life can do to us.

More Mistakes

While at the Playhouse, I was interviewed by the head of the drama department of Duquesne University, a man by the name of Richard Scanga. He signed me up to be an apprentice at the Rabbit Run Summer Theater in Madison, Ohio, where we worked sixteen hours a day and paid *them* fifteen dollars a week!

The good news is sometimes we would be given little parts in plays. Once I played one of four leads in a play, and once I was given a song to sing in a musical revue.

One evening after rehearsal I heard someone from another garage (we had bunks in garages) singing my song, "At the Drop of a Hat." Naively, I thought, "Must be a catchy song." The next day the director called me over and said, "Let's have Jimmy Reilly sing 'At the Drop of a Hat.'" I said, "Jimmy Reilly?" He said, "Yes." I wisely chose not to pursue the conversation.

That was my first experience with being fired in show business, but I don't remember it bothering me. I didn't aspire to be a singer. Later, when I was fired for the one and only time as an actor—well, that was the one exception to the rule regarding how I handled rejection. More about that to come.

The next year they called and asked if I'd like to come back and play a part in a play. They would pay me forty dollars. When I got there, the owner, an older woman, told me the theater had gone union, and she would have to pay me seventy-five dollars, but as they couldn't afford it, she would pay me the seventy-five and I would return thirty-five dollars to her. I was already in rehearsal for the play, and while it felt wrong, I didn't fully comprehend how inappropriate it was.

I was nineteen, and I made a mistake by going along with her. That was in 1954 and I'm writing this in 2008, fifty-four years later, and it still bothers me. I've been told I have a "too scrupulous conscience."

All I can say is since 1954, I've never done anything I considered inappropriate at the time. That doesn't mean that I've never done anything inappropriate. That means my future malfeasance took me years to realize, but I do now.

As I've said, my biggest regret in life is not doing better by my dad as a teenager. I believe the second most serious mistake I've made is also irrevocable. It was in the sixties. There were plenty of girls interested in romance and sex. As I pursued that path, often sleeping with a girl once, sometimes a few days or weeks or even months and moving on, the upset I could be causing never occurred to me. None of these young women told me I had caused them pain, but I now know I did.

Only once did a girl openly express her feelings about my "moving on," and I hadn't even kissed her, held her hand,

or asked her out. It was just an easy chat around a summer stock theater in Pennsylvania. This was in the fifties. I
told her I was heading to Hollywood. She said, somewhat
shocked, "Just like that?" She meant I was abandoning what
she saw as our future relationship.

Who knows what another person goes through? That's
the main reason I've always been nice to everyone. I see all
of us as more or less on the ropes. I want people who meet
me to have a positive experience, but I now realize I hurt
many women in a way I'm truly sorry about.

On the other hand, I've shared these thoughts with cur-
rent close woman friends, and they basically said I'm being
too hard on myself, because the women know what's going
on. I appreciate hearing that, but I still think I was wrong in
a serious way.

Often a man will break up with a woman or a woman
will break up with a man not because they prefer someone
else but because of loyalty and guilt over a prior relationship.
I think it's a good idea not to get involved with someone who
already has a strong involvement, even if they're not pres-
ently seeing that person.

To Hollywood and Back

In 1955, at the age of twenty, I headed to Hollywood with some letters of recommendation from Don Hall, a man connected to the summer theater where I was working. Here's an excerpt from one of them that he wrote to a PR woman.

Here is the story: I have a slight interest in a local summer theater . . . you might say that I dabble at it. . . . This season we secured a young man (20 years old) as a juvenile type. You can believe me, Helen, when I tell you that this kid is not only talented but that he is the most talented young man that I have run across in my 25 years in theatrical work. I would hesitate going any further except that my opinion is backed by almost everyone who has seen him. He never once played a "leading" part this season but people come back week after week to see him. He is tall (6′1″), very nice looking and has a tremendous personality. That is usual for a juvenile, of course. But his talent is most unusual. He can really act. Each portrayal is entirely different and a living, breathing, believable character. And his characterizations are 100%. There is no doubt that this young man will make the grade. It is only a question of where, when and how soon.

Upon meeting me, the PR woman described my impact on entering a room as "About the same as someone who'd just left." Since she felt I had no personal impact, she asked, "What do you do, become the character?" I had no idea what I was doing to elicit the praise in those letters, but attempting with some success to "become the character" *was* what I was doing.

I had a similar letter of recommendation to the head of the talent program at Warner Brothers for whom I did a scene from a popular play and movie at that time, *Tea and Sympathy*. In the story the young man's sexuality is in question, and he has a sexual encounter with an older woman.

Not knowing anything about what such a young man might sound like, I chose to lighten my quality. After the scene was over, the man in charge said, "Have your agent call me." I walked out of the studio on a cloud. "Have your agent call me?!"

Of course, I had no agent, so I went to a phone booth and looked up agents in the Yellow Pages. I actually got one on the phone and told him what had happened. He said he'd call the studio and I should call him the next day, which I did.

I excitedly asked, "What do they want to do with me?" He said, "They don't want to do anything with you. They felt your quality was too light." "Too light? I was doing that for the role," I said, but my explanation fell on deaf ears. I asked the agent if I could come in and meet him, but the answer was a polite no.

If the talent head had engaged me in conversation, he would have seen that my quality wasn't too light. Just as would later happen, I was good enough that he believed that I *was* what they were seeing. Looking back, it was fortunate, because I was better served not being in a studio talent program but learning my craft more, getting experience onstage and in television, and not trying to jump into the movies.

The event that changed my path was that a director I viewed as knowledgeable asked, "What are you doing here? You could become a real actor. You should go to New York and study." So, just like that, I did.

The man's name was John Harding, and I owe him a big debt of gratitude as experience tells me good advice is hard to find in any field. Clearly, very few people give any thought to anyone outside of themselves and family.

In New York, I moved into a room in the Capitol Hall hotel. It had no bathroom, no stove, no hot plate, and no window. It had a sink. As I recall, there were two bathrooms on each floor. Each was shared by about sixteen people.

I was fine. I've always been unusually focused, and I was focused on how to become a good actor, so the lack of accoutrements didn't get to me. Since there was no cooking allowed, and it wasn't financially viable for me to go out to restaurants, I got myself an electric frying pan, which I smuggled past the front desk under my coat. Today I'm *way* more law-abiding.

I hid the electric frying pan under my socks in a drawer. I've always had a lot of socks. No matter what my financial condition was, for some reason I've always had more socks than any one person could wear. Don't get me wrong, I'm not comparing myself to Imelda Marcos and her shoes, but I've always had a lot of socks.

Anyway, in my illegal electric frying pan I would regularly cook chicken wings, which I got for nineteen cents a package. Today, I still eat chicken wings as much as any other food. According to my recent physical, I'm in tip-top shape. I'm not suggesting you run out and get chicken wings; I'm just saying . . .

I think my experience at Capitol Hall—on Eighty-seventh Street between Columbus and Amsterdam in Manhattan—helps me identify with people in shelters. Of course, unlike me, most people in shelters don't have confidence that someday they'll be better than fine. Ironically, Capitol Hall is now a homeless shelter.

I hooked up with my pal from the Playhouse, Julie Ferguson, who had also come to New York to study acting, and we got an audition for the Actors Studio. Julie and I had bonded with one look at the Playhouse as we felt equally silly prancing around the so-called movement class—another concept I have no use for in an acting class. Let it be for aspiring dancers.

I had no idea the Actors Studio auditioned around a thousand people a year and accepted only a few. Julie and I were not among those few. It was the only thing in Manhattan harder to get into than a private preschool.

Uta

Julie and I then auditioned for the legendary acting teacher Uta Hagen and were accepted. I had studied acting for two years, as had Julie—at least. Nevertheless, we were invited to join Uta's beginner's class. I later realized that, generally speaking, acting teachers, like dentists, don't have a high regard for each other. I remember throwing Uta a kiss as we left. I had no way of knowing that would be our last happy exchange for several decades.

Among the things we were asked to do in class was to carry an imaginary suitcase across a room and open an imaginary window. I asked Uta what the purpose of that was. She deeply resented that I would question anything she said and let me know it.

Nevertheless, I couldn't stop myself from asking the question again. This time Uta threatened to throw me out of the class. What made it worse was when I wrote my first book and again said I saw no point in all that imaginary suitcase carrying and window opening.

But I do credit Uta with something she said to me that was very helpful. I was doing a scene in class from the novel

The Catcher in the Rye. When the scene was over, Uta said there was a "pure acting moment" in the scene and asked me if I knew what it was. I had no idea. At one point the actor playing my teacher started to hand me an essay I had written. I reached for it, but he took it back to look at it again. Uta identified that moment as the "pure acting moment," because, as she put it, it was a moment when I didn't know what was happening. That state of not knowing what's coming next is a state good actors aspire to. It's called "living in the moment" and not anticipating what's coming. Learning that concept was very helpful as I tried to unfold what at the time felt like the mystery of acting.

Decades later, Uta was a guest on my cable talk show to promote a book she had written. Even though she had long since dropped those exercises, before the taping began she let me know she still really didn't appreciate my writing about the exercises in a book. I even once spoke at her school and again questioned those exercises, but I don't think Uta heard about it.

It did seem her feelings toward me were somewhat mixed, because she also said that every time her acting studio asked me for a donation, I sent one. I particularly wanted to do that, because she had charged only three dollars a class.

As I've said, because of all my experience in being kicked out of things, Uta threatening to kick me out of class for asking those questions didn't affect me that much. After three years she did say about me, "He questions everything, which is the way it should be."

I saw Uta one more time at a party about a year before

she passed away. She was sitting on a sofa next to a man we both knew, and as I came over to her, she said to the man, "He came into my acting class and acted as though he knew everything." I said, "That certainly wasn't what I was feeling, and I'm really sorry that I offended you." She took my hand and kissed it.

That observation about me acting as though I knew everything came several decades after Uta acknowledged I was right to question whatever I felt was worth questioning. I believe Uta had it right that time. It's the same as in journalism: because we question things doesn't mean we have the answers. America's recent history tells us once again that the problem isn't too many questions but too few.

I have a fantasy that one day I'll be taking a class with Uta in heaven. Once again I'll question something, and once again she'll threaten to throw me out, but it would still be great to see her. If she asked, I'd even carry an imaginary suitcase for her. I can't imagine a need to open an imaginary window, because my fantasy of heaven is that we're outside.

Don't You Dare Show Up!

Recently, I was offered a considerable amount of money just to show up and mingle at a party in Philadelphia. Not to speak. Just to mingle. I couldn't do it. I imagined myself mingling, and I'm sure more than one person there would have asked what brought me there. "Are you a friend of the host?" "No, I've never met him. I'm here because they paid me to come and mingle." I stayed home.

It all brought to mind another time when I was not only *not* paid to show up but told if I *did* show up, I'd be thrown out of the building. When I first came to New York in the fifties, I was able to get a meeting with a major casting director. The woman seemed very pleased to meet me and said I seemed like just the kind of young person she liked to reach out to, a serious, dedicated fellow. I assured her I was, and she said she'd be in touch in a few weeks and would be able to place me in a very small guest role on a popular weekly drama.

I walked out of her office at least one inch off the ground. This was in a period when no one had any interest in placing me in anything, other than on a line to see if there was a cab available for me to drive, which is what I was doing at the time.

On the way to the elevator, I ran into a young woman I knew from Uta's class. She turned out to be working as the casting director's assistant. She seemed surprised to see me, and when I told her of the meeting, she said, "I remember you as someone who took a lot of long pauses when you did scenes in class." She didn't mean it as a compliment. I instantly became uneasy and assured her that I could go as fast as anyone wanted me to, and all those long pauses would certainly present no . . . She didn't seem to be listening, and as she walked away I swallowed hard and said it was really nice to see her.

After about a month of not hearing from the casting director, I called my former classmate and asked if I could take her to lunch. She said she didn't *eat* lunch in such a way that I chose not to ask about dinner.

I let another few weeks of silence from the casting director go by before I wrote what I thought was a very friendly letter reminding her of our meeting and told of meeting her assistant and the pauses issue. I assured her there'd be no problem with pauses and hoped I would still hear from her.

What I heard instead from an agent with whom I was having some conversations was that the casting director told him if I as much as showed up in the lobby of the building where she had her office, she'd have me thrown out!

I showed the letter I had written to a couple of friends to see if I had missed something, but no, it was a pleasant letter from a young man looking for a job. I can only assume that what angered her was it was also a gentle reminder of a broken promise. So it wasn't just teachers who could be abusive.

Later when I was working enough that people had heard of me, I ran into her a couple of times, and she couldn't have been nicer. Neither of us mentioned the past.

Recently, a friend of mine told me this casting director's name came up in a conversation with George C. Scott, and he went ballistic, so evidently her hostile nature was not just visited on me. It's highly unusual when *anything* is personal. If it's happening to you, it's most likely happening to others.

In all this time I've never run into the casting director's assistant, my former classmate. I know she went on to be a producer. If I did run into her, I probably wouldn't recognize her, and if she introduced herself, I'd probably smile and be pleasant to her as well. Oh, I'm not saying I wouldn't slip a long pause or two into our exchange.

A Kiss with
Troubling Ramifications

When I was studying at the Pittsburgh Playhouse, there was one teacher who thought it was humorous to needle me and other students. This whole needling humor thing is tricky. It's, of course, stock-in-trade for many successful entertainers. If you're going to see Don Rickles, for example, it's what you expect. Needling humor that doesn't amuse the person being needled ends up as just mean.

Although I didn't find this teacher particularly amusing, his needling didn't prevent me from basically liking the guy. That's why a couple of years later when I ran into him in New York and he invited me to dinner, I accepted. I was around twenty years old and hardly knew anyone in New York, so I looked forward to the evening.

He invited me to his apartment, and the atmosphere was such that I felt free to say to him that while I always found him to be a nice guy, he might want to take a look at that needling thing. He seemed very appreciative of the observation and correctly took it as a sign that I cared about him. At the end of the evening he said something like, "You're such a sensitive young man. May I kiss you good night?" Still being pretty naïve about this type of thing, I assumed he meant on the cheek. Even though I was uneasy, I tried to appear casual as I said, "Sure." On hearing that, he planted a smacker on my lips. I was stunned, quickly said goodbye, and got out of there.

From the time I was around twelve years old and tried to kiss Myrna Auerbach's cheek in seventh grade, I've never had any doubt about the direction of my sexuality. At the time of the teacher's kiss, I understood so little about what makes a homosexual that I actually wondered if it was like virginity. I knew that if a girl had sex she was no longer a virgin. I wondered if that also meant that being kissed by a man made you a homosexual. I'm still not sure if I was unusually naïve or just normally naïve. My problem was I had no idea where to get the answer to that question. Having no one else to ask, about four months later when I ran into the teacher, I asked *him*. He said, "You're a homosexual if you think you're a homosexual." Well, I knew I wasn't a homosexual, as surely as I knew he was.

In any case, it reminded me of a young woman I had dated when I was around twenty. We didn't have sex, but close, and she asked me if she was still a virgin, and I said, "Absolutely." Still, I had a few tough months when I thought I had lost my heterosexuality.

Years later this man married a famous actress and I did a movie with her, but of course I chose not to tell her that before he kissed her, he had kissed me.

Getting Better
and Getting Banned

Something important was happening to me. I had now been acting for over five years. I had always been doing scenes, getting used to being in front of tough teachers, and in spite of a general lack of encouragement, I was gaining confidence.

I was also fortunate enough in my first year with Uta to become friends with a young woman named Eleni Kiamos who suggested me for a leading role in an off-off-Broadway play where I got a nice notice in a trade paper that led to my getting an agent.

Once I asked my agent's partner if I should have pictures made, and he said, "Sure. Then the people who don't want to see you will know who it *is* they don't want to see."

There was only one place I was working. That was on the Sunday morning dramas on CBS filmed in New York City. Eleni had introduced me to the casting director, who was her friend. With a friend like Eleni you don't need many friends. I seemed to be a favorite over there and only there. One day a group of us gathered around a table for a reading. As I recall there were James Earl Jones, Ossie Davis, and Ruby Dee, among others. After the reading, the producer and director decided they didn't need so many people. They gave five or six actors (not me) twenty-five dollars and thanked them for coming, making at least some feel they weren't good enough. When I saw that, I went to the person responsible for hiring me and said, "This is inappropriate. You really can't do that." She said, "This is the way we do it." I said, "I can't let that happen." She said, "Well, if you want to report it, we'll hire the people, and you'll never work here again," and that's exactly what happened. There's something called principle, and it always came ahead of anything for me when I realized something was wrong, simply because I had no choice. It wasn't that I was such a wonderful person. I simply had no choice.

Mad Men

I started getting parts where I quickly learned that the abuse I got in Uta's class and at the Pittsburgh Playhouse also came from nervous directors. My first live television appearance was on the hour-long *Armstrong Circle Theatre*. It was about the nuclear submarine the USS *Nautilus* going under the North Pole. The director, who had not said anything to me throughout rehearsal, suddenly took me aside close to airtime and angrily said, "If you keep doing what you're doing, you're going to make a fool of yourself—not just yourself but the whole cast—not just the cast but the United States Navy." I had no idea what he was talking about, so I asked. He said, "You're coming off stupid." I have a copy of that show from 1958. I looked at it recently, and unless I drastically changed my performance just before airtime, which I doubt, I'd say the director was coming off hysterically.

I've since heard from others that his behavior toward me wasn't unique. I think most of us have had problems only with people who've had problems with many others. In the 1960s, I auditioned for a Broadway show that was going to be directed by a very famous Broadway director, an icon in the world of comedy. As I came onstage, he shouted to me from the audience, "Charlie Baker [the head of the William Morris Agency's theater department] tells me you're the funniest young actor in New York. Let me see you do something funny!" I made a face, and everyone laughed. Then I began to read for the role. I was about five lines in when the icon called out to me from the back of the theater in what sounded to me like a disgusted voice, "It's a comedy, Charlie!" I stared at him a moment and said, "I know." Needless to say, I didn't get the part, which was eventually given to an excellent young dramatic actor who had never been known for comedy, before or since.

This very successful director came from a school of comedy you most often see today in sitcoms. Set up—joke. Set up—joke. I've never worked liked that. Comedy can come by more than one choice. If you embody the character as best you can, the rhythm most likely will not be set up—joke but will come from the character's natural rhythm, which will vary according to the character.

Directors of the old school not only don't care for this, it alienates them, because they don't understand what's happening.

That wasn't the first time that happened to me. In my second Broadway show, the director of the Rock Hudson and Doris Day movies critically told the leading man, who happily passed it on to me, "I have no idea what Grodin is doing out there," but the audience's response to me made his comment irrelevant.

Early in my career I wrote a piece of material and sent it

to a famous comedian. He graciously responded and said he thought it was funny, but he wrote all his own material. He then added, "Don't make a career out of me." I was never sure if that last line was a joke, but years later I ran into him when he had also become a famous director, and he ranted and carried on quite seriously about how offended he was that he wasn't asked by the studio to direct a movie I had written.

Different versions of that happened over the years. Once in a dramatic role I was supposed to physically assault the great actor Pat Hingle, who was making his first appearance since falling down an elevator shaft in real life. Pat was on crutches, so naturally I was somewhat careful about how aggressively I went after him. The director, a real bully, shouted over the PA system, "You're coming off like a sissy." He also ridiculed James Caan, who did a lot better for himself in the years to come than the director did.

Robert Redford was also in the cast, but I don't remember the director ever yelling at him. There's something about Redford that would discourage that. He and I hung out a bit when we were both in our early twenties. We once went over to the one-room studio he was renting on the Upper West Side of Manhattan. He said the first day he moved in, he opened a closet door to hang up his jacket and found there was a bedroom there!

Lee Strasberg

Through an introduction from my friend Eleni Kiamos, who had become an assistant to Lee Strasberg, I was given an interview. I remember sitting alone with him in his study, and he asked me what actors I admired. I said, "Montgomery Clift, Marlon Brando, and Paul Muni, in his early work." Mr. Strasberg looked at me for the first time and invited me to join his class, I believe because he agreed Mr. Muni was better—less elaborate—in his early work.

Again, I saw no real point in attempting to take an imaginary shower to develop our so-called sensory abilities, but I chose not to say anything. I also didn't understand the emphasis on relaxation exercises. For me, the way to relax is to try to connect to the character and what he's all about and find that person in myself. That will give you something to think about other than the audience, which is the *best* way to relax. I'd rate that as a much better idea than to essentially try to fall asleep in a chair, which is how a lot of teachers teach relaxation, but I chose not to question Mr. Strasberg. Maybe I was finally getting tired of being kicked out. Or maybe it was because I never received any abuse from Mr.

Strasberg. I believe that an exercise that is essentially getting you relaxed enough to fall asleep in a chair is only useful if you'd like to be able to fall asleep in a chair.

Here's an acting exercise I would use if I ever taught, which I won't. I would instruct: Take a bottle of water and empty it into a tall glass, holding it over the glass until absolutely the final drop goes in. The concentration and focus required to be sure you've got that last drop is what's needed in acting.

I would never be interested in teaching acting because to teach suggests that acting is a viable profession to pursue. If kids realized the tiny percentage of people who make a living in show business, at least half the acting schools and drama departments might have to close up shop.

Confidence is an absolute necessity for anyone who appears in front of a camera or large groups of people, and it's certainly necessary to be prepared in every way to have that confidence. It's startling to me how many actors underestimate the importance of being absolutely confident of knowing their lines. Amazingly, in ten years of studying acting I never heard any teacher say that. Some actors believe it's not in their interest to know the lines too soon—they feel it will lead to an interpretation before they're ready. When I say learn the lines early and thoroughly, I'm not talking about interpretation but in the way you would learn to count to ten. The interpretation can come whenever you want, or when the director asks for it. Some English directors insist you show up for the first day of rehearsal knowing the lines. Good idea.

I was obviously getting better, because Mr. Strasberg astonishingly would cite what I was doing as an example of what to do. Once I missed class, and the next week he came over to me and asked if I was okay. That was extraordinary, because in my experience, Lee Strasberg was not a person who reached out. The two most socially uncomfortable people I've ever met are Lee Strasberg and Woody Allen.

I studied with Mr. Strasberg from 1959 to 1962. He must have had thousands of students over the years, and yet in 1975, thirteen years since I had last seen him, on opening night on Broadway of *Same Time, Next Year*, a two-character play I did with Ellen Burstyn, Lee Strasberg was the first person in my dressing room after the show. He said, "You were very good." I asked, "You remember me?" He said, "Of course I do."

After signing a letter saying if I was invited I would accept, I was then invited to join the Actors Studio. It's ironic that the Actors Studio protected itself from rejection, while its members have to deal with it unrelentingly.

Julie

The off-off-Broadway play I was in when I was twenty-one was ominously titled *Don't Destroy Me*. The playwright, Michael Hastings, was English. One night our director told us the agent for the playwright was coming to see the show. The next day the director informed us that after seeing the play the agent had committed suicide. She assured us it had nothing to do with our presentation of his client's play. I completely believed her. I'm sure I'll say this again. Who knows what anyone else is living with?

Another time, the director, a lovely woman who teaches today, told me the celebrated actor Hume Cronyn had seen the play and said of me, "He could be very good, once he gets over his problem." I asked, "What's my problem?" She replied that Mr. Cronyn hadn't said, but she could get his number for me if I wanted to call and ask him.

I imagined the conversation. "Mr. Cronyn, this is Charles Grodin. I understand you saw *Don't Destroy Me* and said I could be very good once I got over my problem. I was wondering . . ." I chose not to call.

After one performance my buddy Julie Ferguson from

the Pittsburgh Playhouse came to see me. We walked down the street after that, and I think I surprised us both when I put my arm around her shoulder.

Julie was very different. Once we were rehearsing a scene at the Playhouse and I suggested we take a break and get a sandwich across the street. She said okay and went into the ladies' room. I went to the men's room, came out, and waited for her outside the ladies' room. After a certain amount of time, I called out her name. There was no answer, so I went across the street to the sandwich shop, where she was sitting at a booth having a sandwich. I went over to her and said, "I thought we were going to get a sandwich." She said without hesitation, "You didn't say with *you*."

After that walk down the street with my arm around Julie's shoulder we eventually became a couple and got married. That's when the trouble started. Not trouble the way we normally think of it—a different kind of trouble. Neither Julie nor I had ever lived with anyone, and it was almost immediately clear that she just wasn't all that comfortable sharing living space with someone. The late comedian Milt Kamen once said the reason he never got married was because when he'd come home there'd be someone in his apartment.

Just after we were married, Julie found a stray dog wandering the streets. She seemed way more comfortable with the dog, which she named Buddy, than with me. (I have a feeling that's not unusual among married couples.) Buddy was a mix of some kind, a nice-looking medium-size dog who Julie brought back to full health. She later worked in an animal shelter.

Julie and Buddy bonded. Buddy seemed to like me considerably less than he liked Julie. When I'd come home he might or might not come over for a pat on the head. When Julie came home he jumped all over her with excitement. As time went on, this behavior continued, except I would describe Buddy's attitude toward me as decreasing to tolerant.

One day as I was walking down the street in Forest Hills, the neighborhood where we lived in the borough of Queens, a pack of dogs approached me menacingly. Not leading the pack but right in the middle was Buddy. I managed to shout them off. After that, Buddy's and my relationship, needless to say, just about disappeared.

Although I never had one, I've always loved dogs. I find it ironic after my experience with Buddy that far and away my two most commercially successful movies were with a dog.

Julie and I never argued. There was just an ongoing withdrawal on her part. Nevertheless, we had a baby, Marion, who is now a wonderful woman. Julie and I persevered. I should say Julie persevered. I had no problem with Julie other than her determination to almost never speak. I once stopped speaking to her to see if she'd notice. It took a few days before she did. Then one day, after about four years without any arguments, Julie took our baby and moved out.

I think a lot of the problem came from Julie's relationship with her mother, who was a fine woman but on the authoritarian side. Julie wanted to be on her own to such a degree that if I took her arm while crossing a busy street she would take it away.

After we separated, we resumed the great friendship we had before getting married. Eventually, she filed for divorce, but we remained close friends—partially, of course, because we had a daughter, but also because we always were great friends.

One day long after our divorce she called to tell me that in the middle of the night something caused her to bolt straight up in bed from a sound sleep. After that happened a few more times she saw a doctor and was diagnosed with a benign brain tumor that the doctor felt should come out. When they operated they found that it was the worst kind of malignant brain tumor, for which there was no treatment. Of course, my daughter and I were devastated.

Marion dropped out of her successful show business career and moved into a house with her mother to be with her during the last three years of her life. I had married again sixteen years after Julie and I were divorced. I had a baby son whom Julie came to see in the hospital when he was born. She was next door receiving chemotherapy. I never heard Julie express any sorrow for herself.

I would sometimes join Marion on Julie's medical appointments. One particularly stands out in my mind. A renowned doctor at New York's Memorial Sloan-Kettering was asking her some questions, which Julie had trouble comprehending due to her gradual loss of faculties. She would look to me for help, and the doctor snapped at her, "Don't look at him! Look at *me*!"

After the examination I complained to officials at the hospital, and that brilliant cancer researcher was then limited only to research—no longer seeing patients. Evidently, I wasn't the first to complain.

Before all this happened and while we were still married, Julie received great acclaim starring in an off-Broadway play. A major agency invited her to meet their agents. At the end of all the meetings, the agent who had brought her in said the feeling was that she wasn't a "commercial" type. This was before actors like Dustin Hoffman and Gene Wilder redefined what a commercial type looked like. Julie looked more like a tomboy, but she had a unique quality that was so special, many of us felt she would become very successful, but that one rejection caused her to stop her pursuit of an acting career. This has been the case for many gifted young actresses and actors who temperamentally could not handle what feels like constant rejection.

After our divorce, Julie became an outstanding woodworker. She made desks and chairs but never charged enough to make a profit, so she also taught woodworking at a Y in New York. She continued this even after her fatal diagnosis. She would be teaching, feel a seizure coming on, excuse herself, walk into the hall, have a seizure, and return to teach.

When she died, she was fifty-two. She was one of a kind and an inspiration for courage.

My daughter later told me she would go home after her visits with me and tell her mother, "Dad's great." Julie would always say, "Yeah, but y'know." Eventually, Marion asked, "Y'know *what*?"

Since it's hard to imagine the mother of a four-year-old child would leave and deprive the little girl of a father, just about everyone thought I left Julie. Even people in my family felt I left my wife and baby. Later a relative of mine who learned the truth said, "I thought that seemed so out of character for you." I once visited Julie and Marion in Pittsburgh. Her father, a distinguished gray-haired man who was the head accountant for Pittsburgh Plate Glass, chose to not even speak to me as he sat in another room reading a paper.

I wonder what he would have thought had he known what actually happened.

In doing research for this book I read a quote from Julie in an interview I came across from 1972, five years after we were divorced. She said of me, "The thing about you is that everything bad about you is right there up front. As you get to know you, you get better and better all the time."

Naturally, I was pleased to read the last part of the quote and honestly baffled by the first part. I hope that's not how everyone perceived me.

Since I've written the above, I've come across an outline for a play I wrote in the early sixties. It's about Julie and me. According to the female character, the male character never stops talking, and a lot of the talking is about sports. The female character has no interest in anything the male character has to say.

In fairness to Julie, that rings true. So when Marion said to Julie, "Dad's a great guy," and Julie said, "Yeah, but y'know," and Marion said, "Y'know *what*?" Julie meant I was always "on" all the time, and Julie was never "on."

Marion, a headlining and brilliant stand-up comedian, makes *me* look like the semistrong silent type. That's why

Marion's experience with me was so different from her mom's. My nickname for Marion as a kid was "Mouth." Julie would say to her, "You're just like your father."

People who prefer silence really shouldn't marry talkative types, and vice versa. Everyone can be a great person, but no relationship is reasonably happy with one person talking most of the time. In defense of us talkers, at least Marion and me, if you want to talk, you'll never get better listeners. If we're with someone in a room, we're comfortable as long as someone is talking, and it doesn't have to be us.

Just before our divorce became final, Julie told Marion, "I think I made a mistake," but by that point we had both moved on. I think she meant yes, I was a talker, but time had taught her she could always count on me. On one hand it was heartbreaking to hear, because my daughter was raised without a dad at home. On the other hand, I wouldn't be married to Elissa for twenty-five years and have my son, Nick, if Julie hadn't left, because I never would have.

Doctors

The doctor who was insensitive to Julie was my first bad experience with a physician but, unfortunately, not the last.

Several years ago, there was a play on Broadway called *The Tale of the Allergist's Wife*. I'll tell you a tale of an allergist. I don't know if this allergist has a wife, but if he does I'll bet she could tell a heck of a tale.

A few years ago I was having an unusually aggressive attack of allergies. I'm fortunate enough to live around a lot of trees. At certain times of the year, and it feels like a *lot* of times, those trees, with all due respect, throw off a lot of pollen, not to mention the pollen thrown off by the bushes and grass. Don't get me wrong. I absolutely hold the trees, the bushes, and the grass in the highest esteem, but sometimes they *do* throw off a lot of pollen, and this time I was sneezing my head off. Hey! Nothing's perfect.

So I asked my local medical office if they could recommend an allergist. I'd never been to an allergist, but the sneezing had gotten to a point that I felt the time had come. My intention was to ask the doctor to suggest something perhaps stronger than the over-the-counter medications I'd been taking for the sneezing.

I sat alone in the waiting room for a while, and then this tall young guy who had shaved his head walked by. He was wearing the white jacket, so I assumed he was the allergist. He was. He didn't even glance at me.

Soon, a nurse appeared, took me into a small room, and asked me to blow into a tube. She made some notes and then disappeared. She came back a few minutes later and said, "The doctor feels you should be able to do better than that." So I gave it all I had. She made some more notes, disappeared again, came back after a few minutes, and said words to the effect that the doctor somehow thought I was cheating.

I assured her I wasn't, and pretty soon the allergist appeared. He probably said hello, but that was it. Clearly, he had little use for small talk or *any* talk about exactly why I was there.

He began looking in my ears, then up my nose, and then down my throat. He still did not say a word. Then he asked me to lie down, took out a stethoscope, and began listening to my heart. Still not a word.

At that point, I considered getting up and walking out, which I'd never done in my life—in a doctor's office, anyway. He looked at me very solemnly and said, "I hear a murmur." I looked at him and said, "I've been examined regularly since I was born, and no one has ever said that." He said, "I'm a musician, and I have a very keen sense of hearing. Some murmurs are meaningless, and some aren't." He suggested I see a cardiologist.

Still not one word about my sneezing. I said some things to him I've blocked out—no profanity, but I walked out and drove over to my internist, who briefly examined me and said, "You have a negligible murmur which isn't even worth mentioning."

I did go to a cardiologist, who said, "You have a negligible murmur which isn't even worth mentioning."

Rather than go to another allergist about the sneezing, which *was* worth mentioning, I decided to continue to sneeze. I figured there were a lot worse things than sneezing, and I'd just experienced one. Oh, yeah, the allergist wrote me a letter about six months later that I tore up without opening. What goes around really does come around.

In fairness to the allergist, I've since been told by a very good source that he has an excellent reputation, which just proves again there's always at least two sides to everything.

I can't end this story without saying a few hundred words about the cardiologist, who also concluded, "You have a negligible murmur which isn't even worth mentioning." (That's probably why my regular doctors chose not to mention it.)

First, I met with the guy. He didn't examine me. We had a pleasant chat, and he scheduled me for an echocardiogram, which reveals if a murmur is worth mentioning or not. His was a big cardiac practice, and I assume he just didn't get my message that I needed to change the appointment because that was the day my eighteen-year-old son was to have his first scene in a movie. I wouldn't be on the set, but I'd definitely be somewhere in the building.

Evidently, the cardiologist only heard I had changed the appointment, not the explanation. Although it's a busy office, he shouldn't have sent a letter, which I received on a Saturday, citing several reasons why I might not survive the weekend! It was such a frighteningly provocative letter, I chose to share it with no one, not even my wife—*especially* not my wife.

I called the physician on Monday and made an attempt to put a little lighter spin on his letter, but he interrupted me by asking, "What's the first part of the paper you read every day?" I said, "The front page." He said, "I read the obituaries." We scheduled an appointment for the next day. It turns out, as I've said, that I have a negligible heart murmur that isn't worth mentioning. I hope he reads this and takes a good look at himself. I think that's good advice for all of us.

He called me about four months later, but I told his secretary I wouldn't take his call and explained why.

I don't ever recall not taking someone's call to that point, but I was provoked to do it again within the past year. The son of a girl I went to high school with reached out to me. He's a journalist and wanted me to see some things he'd written. He sent them to me, but I found them so hateful toward women that I had my assistant e-mail him that my experience with women was so different from his that I was really not his audience. Obviously insulted, he e-mailed back that he didn't need me to be part of his audience, because he already had a huge audience. Then he e-mailed and asked if I would call a big speaker's bureau head on his behalf. My assistant e-mailed him that to me that call would indicate support.

He then called me, and I didn't take the call. Even for someone who likes to say yes to people, enough is enough.

The only other weird experience I'd ever had with a doctor occurred a few decades ago when I went in for a checkup and the doctor asked me how many women I'd been with. I asked him the relevance of the question, and he absolutely couldn't answer.

He just stared at me and said, "There are a lot of weird people in your profession." I looked at him and said, "There are a lot of weird people in *your* profession."

Most recently, I went to a doctor to treat an ear infection and he wanted to operate on me for a brain tumor that an MRI at Yale revealed I didn't have. Actually, I had no tumor anywhere and easily got rid of the ear infection with antibiotics, needless to say prescribed by another doctor.

Several years ago I was seated next to a Harvard scholar at a dinner party. The reason the host chose to sit me next to him was that the man had been told by a prominent doctor that he had six months to live because of a malignant brain tumor.

The host, knowing my experience with Julie and her brain tumor, sat me next to him. The man told me what had happened to him, and all I said was, "If you walk across the street to another hospital you may hear something entirely different." Amazingly, he seemed completely taken aback by what I said. Well, he walked across the street and many more streets, and twenty years later, he's alive and well.

When it comes to a serious medical diagnosis, never assume that what someone tells you, no matter who it is, is the final answer.

One last thought on doctors. Some but not all let their patients know they're due for something. Every conscientious doctor should do that. Then, if something happens, it won't be because the doctor didn't do his full job.

The Woman in the Hotel

When I was around twenty and studying acting in New York, I lived in the building I described earlier that is now a homeless shelter.

I had a job working as a night watchman on the Brooklyn waterfront for the Pinkerton Detective Agency. I worked from midnight to eight at Todd's Shipyards. My job was to patrol, in full uniform, empty warehouses and call in if I saw a fire or anything. I wasn't armed, and somehow I happily never considered what "anything" might be. I was paid $1.62 an hour. I was paid a dollar an hour for guard work in Manhattan.

One day, before I got together with Julie and was living in my room with no window, I was walking through the lobby of the building (I wasn't in uniform) and was approached by a woman who seemed about fifteen years older than I was who also had a room in the building. I had never seen her before, but she walked up to me, said hello, and told me her therapist thought it would be good for her if she had sexual relations, and I seemed like a clean-cut young man. Nothing even remotely like that ever happened to me before or since.

I told her it was true. I was clean-cut, and I agreed to come to her room later.

I went back to my room, thought about it, and something told me maybe this wasn't such a good idea. I didn't have a girlfriend at the time, but it all felt too strange, so I knocked on her door about a half hour before the appointed time. She answered it wearing a dressing gown. I explained I had to go to work. She nodded, and that was that.

Years later, I ran into her on the street, chatted a moment, and made a date. This was in a period when Julie and I were separated, but I still had some hope we'd get back together. She came to where I was living, and . . .

About a month later she called to tell me she was pregnant. I had taken precautions, but nevertheless there it was.

I have seldom been so distraught. In my brief encounter with this woman it was clear she might have had more than a few emotional issues and had even been institutionalized, but even now, growing up in the era that I did, I believe if you get a woman pregnant, you should marry her. I was unable to dissuade myself from that belief, even under those strange circumstances. It also meant the definitive end of my marriage, which had already ended, but I hadn't fully accepted it.

I walked the streets of Manhattan for weeks in a terrible state. Then, one day I got a call from her saying she wasn't pregnant after all, just "late."

I actually went to see her to look at her face-to-face to confirm that it was true. I completely believed her and moved on with my life, although for a long time when the phone rang, which it hardly ever did, I feared for a moment it was her saying there was a baby. Thankfully, that call never came.

Many years later I found myself in bed with a beautiful actress. When I brought up the subject of birth control, neither of us had any. I got dressed and, I hope politely, took my leave. To this day, that woman resents me. I understand, but since, as I've said, I believe marriage must follow a pregnancy, I had no choice. I also believe in a woman's right to choose simply because, as many have said, if a woman wants an abortion somehow she will get one, and if *Roe v. Wade* is ever repealed, abortions obviously would be done under less than safe circumstances.

Grammar school basketball team. I'm standing on the right.
Are we serious enough? (Author's Collection)

My grandmother and
me in Pittsburgh in the
early fifties.
(Author's Collection)

My family. My dad is standing on the far right.
My mother is sitting on the far right. My grandfather has the
beard, and my grandmother is to his left. I'm standing behind
my grandfather—always a good place to stand.
(Author's Collection)

Entering the University of Miami, after my dad died.
(Author's Collection)

My daughter, Marion, contemplating going into show business.
(Author's Collection)

My daughter, Marion,
who's a headlining stand-up comedienne in New York.
(Author's Collection)

By this time in the sixties, I had a window.
(Author's Collection)

My one indiscretion. She was irresistible.
(Author's Collection)

My mother, who radiated love toward me.
(Author's Collection)

Roger Ailes, who now runs the Fox Cable Network, produced
this special when he ran CNBC. From left to right, Phil Donahue,
Bob Berkowitz, Sheila Stainback, Vladimir Pozner, Cal Thomas,
me, Dick Cavett, Al Roker, Mary Matalin, Tim Russert,
and Geraldo Rivera. (Author's Collection)

It's so sad that Johnny Carson, who brought joy to so many,
didn't experience more of it in his own life. (Author's Collection)

David Letterman at least knows I'm kidding.
(Author's Collection)

Roger Ailes and me. (Photo by Steve Friedman)

Democratic Senator Edward Kennedy and Republican Senator Orrin Hatch. I hosted a benefit at Ethel Kennedy's home at Hickory Hill. Senator Kennedy and Senator Hatch sang the song "Together" from *Gypsy*. It was the hit of the evening. (Author's Collection)

I so admired all of them. From left to right, me, Bob Simon, Vicki Mabrey, Dan Rather, Scott Pelley, and Charlie Rose. (Photo by Larry Busacca and John Filo/CBS)

Joy and Regis Philbin, and me. I told Regis I had in my possession a photo of Joy that would get her movie stardom, but I wanted a percentage before I'd hand it over. We're negotiating. (Author's Collection)

From left to right, Elizabeth Wilson, me, Paul Newman,
Joanne Woodward, Eli Wallach, Anne Jackson.
(Photo by Kathleen O'Rourke)

Bob Ellis, Eli Wallach, me, and Jack Klugman.
(Photo by Steve and Anita Shevett)

Brandon Hein. He was taken into custody when he was eighteen, and he was sentenced to life with no chance of parole. He's now thirty-one. He didn't kill anyone or steal anything. That's America's disgrace: the felony murder rule. (Author's Collection)

Arlene Oberg comes out of prison with her arm around her daughter Lisa. Arlene died of a heart attack in her thirties. (Author's Collection)

Elaine Bartlett embracing her oldest son, Apache, as she's released from prison. It was Elaine's case that provoked New York legislators to reform the Rockefeller drug laws, gaining an early release for approximately 1,000 people. (Author's Collection)

Elaine Bartlett, Jan Warren, Arlene Oberg.
(Author's Collection)

Randy Credico and
me. Randy leads me to
victims of our system.
He is my hero.
(Author's Collection)

Candid Camera

In the sixties I was hired by Allen Funt to be a writer and director for *Candid Camera*. I'm still not sure exactly why he hired me. I know he had liked me in a Broadway show he had seen, but I had played a nerdy Wharton Business School graduate, nothing that would suggest I'd be good for *Candid Camera*.

A young agent, Owen Laster, who went on to become a major literary agent, set up a meeting with Mr. Funt. I don't remember anything that transpired at the meeting. All I know is I was hired and given my own film unit.

There was a slight hitch, though. I had been asked to go to Hollywood to be on a soap opera, *The Young Marrieds*. I had no interest in doing that, having worked for a short time in New York on a soap opera called *Love of Life*, which was the most difficult thing I'd ever done. It really was a challenge to memorize so many lines each day. I felt if I read the teleprompter it would look like I was reading a teleprompter—not exactly a good career move. I couldn't get anywhere near the level of acting I was capable of, because there simply wasn't enough time to be confident enough with the lines, so it would be next to impossible to embody the character. I don't watch soaps or much of anything on television besides news and sports, but I'm sure there are some actors and actresses on soap operas who, after playing their character for years, do it a lot better than I did.

I accepted the job on *The Young Marrieds* because I had a six-year-old daughter and bills to pay. I said I'd only do it for six months and was surprised when they accepted that. It was there I met Ted Knight, who later played Ted Baxter on *The Mary Tyler Moore Show.*

Ted played my boss on *The Young Marrieds,* and it was almost impossible for us to act the soap opera story together as it was a variation of the same scene over and over, which reduced us both to helpless laughter throughout rehearsal, much to the chagrin of the people in charge. I loved Ted. Once I was driving down a steep hill in Los Angeles with him and the car's brakes failed. In order not to go over a cliff, I crashed the car into a brick wall of a garage. Amazingly, neither one of us was hurt. Ted passed away years later after refusing chemotherapy for what I assume was incurable cancer.

It was at his house at a gathering after he passed that I met Dabney Coleman. Dabney and I are close to this day, decades later. I wish I could have spent time with Dabney and Ted together, if even for one night. Sadly, it never happened.

After my six months were up, I headed back to New York and *Candid Camera* and immediately ran into an unforeseen obstacle in the person of an executive who worked under Allen who seemed to openly resent that I had been hired without her knowledge.

She met with me alone in an office and wanted to hear my ideas. I'd had six months to think about it, so I had about twenty-five I presented to her. She responded to each with variations of, "I don't like it. That won't work. We've done something like that. No. No. No," and more noes. Then she sat back in her chair and looked at me, I guess to see if I would just leave the building. She obviously had no idea she was dealing with a thirty-one-year-old who had overcome being impeached at ten.

I said, "I know I can be wrong, but I don't believe I can be wrong twenty-five times in a row." It was decided we should go see Allen Funt, *after* she had expressed her feelings about me to him. Allen had just emerged from a Jacuzzi or a sauna, and he was sitting on a table wrapped in a towel. He asked me what I thought was my best idea. I told him, and he told me to do it.

The idea was that I was a young aspiring singer from Pittsburgh, and my uncle, played by the late Joey Faye of vaudeville fame, would tell a professional singing coach that he promised his late sister, my mother, that he would back me in a singing career, but he wanted a professional's judgment of my potential.

We paid a coach for the use of his studio, and the coach called about six other coaches, telling them he had to be out of town and asking if they could come over to hear this young man and give their judgment. I believe we paid each one twenty dollars. Again, this was the 1960s. We scheduled them about an hour apart so they wouldn't run into each other.

The studio was rigged with hidden cameras and mikes. The piano player, of course, was with us, and I burst into a completely sincere but way less than mediocre version of a somewhat operatic piece called "Be My Love," made famous by Mario Lanza.

All day long the coaches were stunned, surreptitiously glancing at the piano player and Joey Faye, both of whom acted as though something reasonably acceptable was coming out of me.

A middle-aged heavyset male coach just stared at me as I sang, stunned. When I finished, I said, "I did this song for a group of Shriners in Pittsburgh and got a standing ovation! Of course, I didn't do it as well as I just did it now." The coach said, "I wonder what the hell *that* sounded like?"

One woman coach said to me indignantly, "I manage a baritone whom the *New York Times* has called one of the ten finest singers in this country, and *this man cannot make a living*!" I looked at her a moment and asked, "Does he have my range?"

Their outrage was hilarious. I went back to my office feeling great. The phone rang, and it was my agent. He said, "Congratulations!" I thought, "Wow, good news travels fast," but I soon realized he was being facetious. He then said, "You're fired." "I'm fired?" He said, "You set a record. *Candid Camera* is *known* for firing people, but nobody ever got fired on the first day."

Evidently, a couple of coaches had already threatened lawsuits, and Allen Funt was very upset with me. I went to see him and asked him to look at the footage to see how funny it was, even though we couldn't show the segment. He did and rehired me.

I did some good work after that. Once we took over a sightseeing bus in New York, and Joey Faye described the sights of what we called the Garage and Warehouse Tour. The bus drove up and down streets filled only with garages and warehouses, and Joey would say things like, "Trucks come here every day and load up with supplies that are taken to stores around the city." The camera was on the passengers, who were growing more and more agitated. Suddenly, an English fellow called out, "Where's the Empire State Building?! Where's the U.N.?" and Joey said, "The Garage and Warehouse Tour is our most popular tour."

Another time we took over a New York restaurant called Voisin. Every time someone would take a sip of water, I would rush over and fill their glass. If there were any crumbs on the table, I would swoop in and sweep them off. Then I'd go back and listen with my headset to their comments, which began with, "Boy, they have some service here," and then changed to, "This is starting to get on my nerves." Ironically, when we announced we were from *Candid Camera*, no one would sign a release, because at every table we had miked, people were with someone they weren't supposed to be with.

After a short time Allen asked me to go out to Kennedy Airport and put up a fake men's room door. I told him I didn't think it would lead to comedy when people came off a plane wanting to use a bathroom and then couldn't. That shoot was a disaster, and I was notified at the airport that a call had come in from the *Candid Camera* office saying I was fired again. I chose not to go see Allen and remind him I had been against the idea in the first place.

Years later, after I had directed an Emmy-winning television special, my agent got a call from *Candid Camera* asking if I'd be interested in directing a special they were doing, but I declined. The lesson was, don't ever accept a job from someone who has already fired you twice.

Endings

The first Broadway show I acted in was a standing room only hit in the early '60s called *Tchin-Tchin*. It starred Anthony Quinn and the great English actress Margaret Leighton. I played the supporting part of Margaret Leighton's son. The play had only three speaking roles.

I got excellent reviews but wasn't offered another Broadway show for about two years. Part of the reason was that I played an unusual character—a mama's boy—and I evidently did it well enough that people thought I *was* a mama's-boy type. My take-home pay in the play was $107 a week. I had a wife and baby, and since the play was such a big hit and I had gotten rave reviews, I asked the production supervisor if he would ask the general manager if I might have a slight raise.

When I didn't hear anything for about a month I assumed the answer was no, but the production supervisor said, "He didn't say no." I said, "Really?" He said, "He didn't say no. He just laughed."

Years later, when I became known and the general manager became a producer, he sent me a play to be in. I chose not to read it. What goes around does come around.

Something really unexpected happened after the opening night performance of *Tchin-Tchin*. I was with Julie and two of our closest friends, a couple we had met in acting class. The woman said to me at one point, "You've been talking about yourself for twenty minutes." It *was* opening night of my first Broadway show, and talking about it for twenty minutes in my mind doesn't exactly qualify as a federal offense.

My friendship with that woman came to a mutual end that evening. It later ended with my male friend as well when they got married. I believe if I hadn't made it to Broadway, as they hadn't, we'd still be friends.

In the second Broadway show I did, I became close friends with another actor, who was considerably older than I was. That friendship came to an end when he saw an ad for *The Heartbreak Kid* in the paper. I had chosen to not even mention to him that I had starred in a movie, properly guessing it would end that friendship.

Something very uncharacteristic of me happened when I was a commentator for *60 Minutes II*. At the end of my first year, I told the head man, Jeff Fager, who now runs *60 Minutes*, that I wanted to replace my producer. I also said I would only do this if he could be sure she would be placed elsewhere at CBS. He said that could be done and then asked me why I wanted to replace the woman he had suggested to me. I said I wanted a producer who wasn't also a second editor.

Jeff, as well as being a terrific guy, is also obviously an excellent editor and an all-around brilliant producer who's on fire with his work. He's won more awards than I can count.

Once Jeff signs off on a piece, you don't want further editorial notes. No one should have more than one editor.

I remember more than a few times after Jeff had signed off on a piece, my producer continued to give me further editorial notes, even after I asked her not to. I said, "You expect me to go back to Jeff? Thanks, but no thanks." Producing is a full-time job, and one she did very well, and that's what I needed.

Two other events caused me to want to make a change. Once I brought in my résumé for her to read so she could see I wasn't exactly someone who'd gone from being a movie actor to a commentator on *60 Minutes II*. It listed five years at CNBC and MSNBC doing commentary, not to mention producing and directing television specials that either won an Emmy or were nominated. I'd been deeply involved with those scripts and in charge of the editing after the filming was completed. When we completed *Heaven Can Wait*, Warren Beatty asked me to be involved with the editing. (I didn't put that on the résumé. It wouldn't have mattered to her anyway.)

I'd also written movies, produced, written, and directed plays in New York, and written several books, not to mention writing pieces for the *New York Times* and several magazines. I had produced and directed a Simon and Garfunkel special for CBS when she was working there as a receptionist. As she looked at my résumé, she openly rolled her eyes, making no effort to conceal her disdain. Not a good idea.

The clincher came when I asked her to show Jeff a piece I had done without a special effect and asked her to ask him if he felt we needed it. Jeff called and asked if *I* felt we needed the special effect. I asked, "How was it shown to you?" He said, "*With* the special effect." Neither he nor I felt we needed it, but the producer went against what I thought was my clear request and showed it to Jeff that way because she wanted it. That sealed it for me. She is a very nice woman, but she was way out of line. I believe she could read this now and still not get it.

The second year, Jeff suggested a nice young fella he had worked with to be my producer, and the exact same thing happened, with continued editorial suggestions after Jeff had signed off on a piece. At one point, this young man said to me, "I feel as though you're standing on my neck." Even though I told him several times, he just couldn't grasp that once Jeff signed off on these two-minute pieces, that was sufficient for me.

If you're the on-camera person, it's just not in your interest to know your producers would like you to use their words, not yours. Not to be overly redundant, but it's a distraction.

I went to this fella's wedding, and when he introduced me to his mother I have never been greeted more coldly, a perfect example of someone acting on hearing one side of a story. Of course, it was understandable. It is so difficult for a parent to be cordial to someone who has caused their kid upset, no matter what the bigger picture might clarify.

By the start of my third season, Jeff and I agreed that the young woman who had been more than capably serving as my associate producer would be perfect as my producer. She was content with producing and didn't editorialize after the pieces were okayed by Jeff, and she *was* perfect.

But then came a week when Jeff chose not to run my piece, and I resigned, just as many a newspaper columnist has after similar circumstances. My rationale was if there was an option of my piece not running, it could happen on any given week.

I could have lived with that as well, but these commentaries were all I was doing, because my contract called for total exclusivity—meaning I couldn't do movies, which I was being asked to do, or commentary elsewhere, which I was asked to do on what was then called Court TV. Henry Schleiff, then head of Court TV, made the point to Jeff that I had a substantial cable following that would help build a following on *60 Minutes II*, but Jeff wasn't buying that argument.

Looking back, I think I made a mistake in at least not giving the broadcast notice instead of leaving immediately, as the then head of CBS News, Andrew Hayward, a very good man, asked of me. I should have realized that when a columnist for a newspaper resigns, there are other columnists there. Of course, I was the only commentator on *60 Minutes II*. I was and am so fond of Jeff Fager, I now feel I owed him that. All these years later we remain friends and talk on the phone from time to time, which I so enjoy.

Oddly enough, the experience at *60 Minutes II* that really sticks in my mind didn't involve Jeff or my two producers.

Once when I was working with an editor on one of my pieces, I gave him some notes that would take ten minutes or so to execute, so I walked out of the small editing room to go back to my office, which was at the end of a long hall and around a corner. As I stepped right outside of the editing room, I saw for the first time a large lounge area with lots of windows and TVs. No one was there, so I walked in, sat down, and turned on the news.

In a few minutes, a man appeared and sat across the room. After a moment, he said to me, "Doesn't your office have a window?" I said, "No. Actually my office doesn't have a window." He said, "This is the editors' lounge." I said, "Oh, okay," got up, and as I left saw a sign that read EDITORS' LOUNGE. Oddly, there were no correspondents' or commentators' lounges. I went to my windowless office and knew I had a story worth telling.

I can't even imagine what Andy Rooney would have said if an editor said that to him, but on the other hand no editor or anyone anywhere would ever say something like that to Andy.

All in all, the *60 Minutes II* experience was wonderful, and I'll always be grateful to Jeff Fager for giving me the opportunity.

When I left the broadcast, I sent an e-mail to everyone saying how much I would miss them—even the editor who wouldn't let me sit in the editors' lounge.

Special Agents

In my second Broadway show I again played an unusual character, the nerdy Wharton Business School graduate with glasses and bad posture, and the same thing happened as in my first Broadway play. People assumed that was what I was like.

Joe Schoenfeld, who was cohead of the William Morris Agency's movie department, came backstage to say hello to me after the show, and when I opened the dressing room door, he saw someone without the glasses and the bad posture and said, "I'm looking for Charles Grodin." That moment began an important relationship with Joe, who I believe was about thirty years older than I was. He became a real promoter of mine.

My biggest promoter was Harry Ufland, who had asked Joe to go backstage to meet me. From the time Harry became my agent in the early sixties, he never stopped telling everyone, "Charles Grodin is as good as it gets no matter what he does." Harry's in my will.

Joe Schoenfeld was second only to Harry. I once went to his office to ask if he had any advice for me. I was a guest star on television shows about a half-dozen times a year, which grossed me six thousand dollars—a thousand a show. This was 1966.

Even though I was considered a successful and highly regarded young actor, I had gone from making $7,000 a year on Broadway in 1962 to $6,000 a year on television in 1967. (A lot of big movie stars of the forties and fifties died broke.) Again, I had a wife and child. I asked Joe if he had any thoughts. As he pondered my question, his phone rang. A picture shooting in Yugoslavia called *Castle Keep* with Burt Lancaster and others was having some problems. Joe represented a number of the principals involved. Millions of dollars were at stake.

After the call, I said to Joe, "I see you have much bigger issues to deal with. I'll come by on another day." He said, "Not at all, Chuck, this happens all the time. Please go on."

There are not a lot of people I will always cherish, but Joe Schoenfeld, who has been deceased for years, remains in my thoughts.

Another time, the legendary Abe Lastfogel joined Joe and me for a drink in Joe's office at the end of the day. At some point, Abe said, "Why don't we go into my office and have our drink under Johnny's picture." Johnny was Johnny Hyde, who was Abe's partner when William Morris really became William Morris, around 1930.

I have no point to make in the following two stories about two other William Morris agents I knew in the sixties, one in California and the other in New York, but I think they're worth telling.

Cy Marsh was a flamboyant Hollywood agent who actually stood on his desk as he talked to me. I was asking if he could help get me considered for bigger television shows.

He proclaimed, while standing on his desk, "I represent Rod Steiger." Compared to Rod Steiger of *On the Waterfront* fame, I was relatively unknown. Cy said, "How am *I*, who represents Rod Steiger, going to look if I ask, 'Anything for Charles Grodin?'" I found him hilarious, even though I don't think he *ever* asked, "Anything for Charles Grodin?"

Rod Steiger was a guest on my cable show in the nineties about thirty years after Cy talked to me standing on his desk, which I assume looking back must be some kind of power move. It wasn't obvious at the time. The power move I *do* find obvious is when people in positions of authority speak in something slightly above a whisper in a private office. I have some hearing loss. But not that much. They speak in something slightly above a whisper.

Anyway, Rod Steiger was on my show thirty years later. I was doing a program on depression, and he was one of three or four guests who battled that terrible scourge. My mother and my brother have both suffered from depression, so I obviously don't mean to be funny, but Rod Steiger was so depressed on the show that even though he wasn't with me in the studio but was on the satellite, *I* started to get depressed.

The agent for William Morris in New York who was Harry Ufland's boss when he and I first connected observed of me, "He's probably going to be another Eli Wallach, but who's got the time?"

This agent was widely known for reaching for any male's scrotum that came within his reach. He never made that move on me—something about my attitude, I guess. On the few occasions when he called me, I felt I better take a pill of some kind, because his energy was so high. He died young. Call me crazy; I liked him, too. Characters! I've often said sometimes the agents should be the performers!

Critics

A critic for *Variety*, Art Murphy, who called himself Murph, said of me in my second leading role in a movie in 1974, "It would be sad to think an acting career lay ahead." The next year, I won a best actor award on Broadway in *Same Time, Next Year*, and the year after that I was in *Heaven Can Wait*. That critic is now deceased. When articles appeared about him after his passing, it was reported he was snappish around the office and enjoyed dressing in women's clothes.

I honestly don't look down on how anyone dresses, as long as they're properly covered. Snappish around the office or anywhere is *way* over the line to me.

I'm more sympathetic to a local critic in Santa Monica who said of a movie I wrote, *Movers & Shakers*, "If you want to know what it feels like to die sitting upright in your theater seat, go see this movie." The late ABC critic Joel Siegel said of the same movie, "You'll laugh till you cry."

While I don't believe it was as good as Joel Siegel said, I obviously don't agree with the Santa Monica critic. It probably never occurred to him that the movie was too hip or inside for him to get. I mean, *I* don't get a lot of things, and I almost always believe it's my shortcoming.

I mean, how bad could the movie be? The cast included Walter Matthau, Steve Martin, Gilda Radner, Bill Macy, Penny Marshall, and Tyne Daley, among many others who've had a job or two, including me. Inside? Yes. Bad? No.

One of my closest friends was a critic, Richard Watts, Jr. From the early seventies until he died at the age of eighty-two in 1980, Dick was the theater critic for the *New York Post* and before that a movie critic and later a theater critic for the *New York Herald Tribune*. He and I and a changing group of three or four others would meet every Friday night at Manhattan's "21" Club for drinks and then have dinner there or go to other restaurants around the city. I loved Dick Watts. He was as kind a man as I've ever met and knowledgeable on so many subjects.

The late Clive Barnes, formerly the drama critic of the *New York Times* and later a critic for the *New York Post*, wrote about Dick after he passed. He said among other things that Dick's opinions were informed by knowledge, love, and, very significantly, compassion. He said his writing was modest, and he had the honesty almost to protest his subjectivity.

Dick once gave a mixed review to something I had produced and directed on Broadway. He said that most likely part of his problem with the play came from some hearing loss he was suffering, as there were a number of lines spoken offstage. That Friday at "21," I read into his ear a review from another major critic. He listened carefully, and when I finished turned to me with a big grin and said, "Why, Chuck, that's a *rave!*"

There was only one Dick Watts. He knew he was subjective, as we all are, and he genuinely came to the theater wanting to like the production.

Maybe, in fairness, all critics want to like what they're reviewing. Personally, I couldn't handle going to see a play or a movie five nights a week or so. I mean, I'd come *in* in a bad mood, and that of course wouldn't be fair to the people putting on the show.

The Graduate

No matter how many times I've written about or said to people that I did not turn down the lead in *The Graduate*, the question always comes up in interviews. "Why did you turn down the lead in *The Graduate*?"

I had read about twenty pages from the script for the director, Mike Nichols; the writer, Buck Henry; and the producer, Larry Turman; with an excellent actress reading the role of Mrs. Robinson. Mike called me that night to say, "You're our number one choice. We don't have a second choice." He also said, "When I close my eyes and listen to you, you're perfect, but when I look at you . . ." It was a typically gracious Mike way of saying, "Lose some weight." It wasn't that I was heavy, he just thought that being thinner would make me look younger. I was thirty-one. The character was supposed to be early twenties. He said they wanted to do a screen test, but only for "photographic purposes."

In order to do a screen test you must first agree to the fee they will pay you, if they choose to hire you. They offered me $500 a week to star in *The Graduate*, plus a seven-year contract with modest increases, all with their option, of course. I was making more than that for a three-day guest spot on a television show, and I simply thought it was unfair. It really had nothing to do with the money, but the fairness.

This attitude, which first reared its head on the CBS Sunday morning shows, manifested again. Even though I have sometimes worked for scale in really low-budget movies, in this case I thought the salary was inappropriate, and I still feel that way. We went back and forth and finally agreed on a thousand dollars a week.

It seemed that within an hour my doorbell rang, and somebody delivered a large packet of pages from *The Graduate* that they wanted me to memorize before going in front of the cameras the next morning. That's the kind of thing you deal with if you're doing a soap opera, but to get to the level of acting they had seen me do in the office reading the script would be impossible. A note enclosed in the envelope read, "If you have any questions, call Mike Nichols," and they gave me his home phone number.

Now I believe he might have subconsciously known something wrong was happening. I called him and said, "With this many pages to memorize overnight, I can't be at the level I know you'd expect." By then, I had studied acting for ten years and done a lot of theater and television. He again said, "Don't worry about it. It's only a photographic test," and alluded to my need to lose weight to look younger. When I showed up on the set I had lost so much weight that Mike didn't recognize me. However, it wasn't only a "photographic test."

I absolutely didn't know the lines. I asked if I could improvise. The answer was no, and when Mike asked me if I would jump up and down on the bed and I asked why, it confirmed his feeling, a false one, that I would be difficult to deal with. *I was not offered the role.* I thought the whole thing was handled inappropriately. I'm sure that none of the people behind *The Graduate* realized that. I know Mike and Buck, and they're really nice guys. Later, when I did work with Mike on *Catch-22*, he discovered what everyone learned when they worked with me: I wasn't difficult to deal with.

One director who probably wouldn't agree with that last statement is Joel Schumacher, who directed *The Incredible Shrinking Woman*, which I believe was his first picture. It was a movie filled with special effects, which by definition meant there would be more than your average mind-numbing hours of waiting around—like, eight. I wanted to make sure I wasn't the only one who felt some thought could be given to how many hours the actors were waiting. I not only wasn't the only one, but one actress actually felt it was being done deliberately to drive her crazy!

I went to Joel to ask if he could give some consideration to the actors' call times. He looked at me as though I was nuts. He said, "You expect me to think about *that*!?" It was clear the special effects were more than enough of a challenge for him. I said, "I *do* expect you to think about that." He told me that I was being paid more than Lily Tomlin, who played the Shrinking Woman. I said, "Really? Who's her agent?"

Then I said, "Under your logic the person being paid the most should wait the longest." He said, "You're like a Jewish prince." Joel is Jewish, so I didn't take it as an anti-Semitic remark, but I didn't like it. Joel saw the look in my eye that surfaces from time to time and quickly added about himself, "And I'm white trash."

Back to *The Graduate*. Turn it down? I may be a lot of things, but nuts really isn't one of them. At the time, in spite of working in television, I owed $800 to the Actors Federal Credit Union. Believe me, I didn't turn down *The Graduate*. To this day, I don't think they realize they made it impossible for me to succeed. I say that not to point a finger but for directors in the future who may not realize what actors need to be at their best.

For example, when I'm involved in casting plays I write, instead of having the director, producer, casting director, and myself sit behind a long table, I give the person auditioning a table to sit behind as well, instead of just a straight-back chair. Sometimes I give them my table.

There's a reason plays are in rehearsal for four weeks and then in previews before critics come. Movie scripts are often given to actors months ahead of time. As I've said, the only place actors are asked to memorize pages and pages of dialogue in a short period is on soap operas. I've done two soap operas and found it impossible to be anywhere near the level I can reach with the time given in movies and onstage. There are wonderful soap opera actors, but you don't ever hear their names mentioned among our great actors. When they had opportunities with movies or theater they could really fulfill their potential.

I once asked a veteran soap opera actress if she enjoyed the work. She said, "The only thing I enjoy is the last line."

I've always tried to focus on what I *have* and not on what I don't have, because in the overall scheme of things, if I consider what I have been given it would be ridiculous for me to ever feel sorry for myself, and I never have.

I've known Mike Nichols for forty years, but since *The Graduate* test I've never had a bumpy moment with him. Whenever I see him, I can't help but be aware I'm looking at someone very special—so original in his wit and so smart—probably in a class of his own, at least in show business. The two of us once had lunch, and the subject of *The Graduate* never came up. Oddly, I don't even remember thinking about it when I was with him.

In 1997, thirty years after our awkward, failed encounter on *The Graduate*, Mike called to compliment me on something he'd seen on my cable show—a classy move. He's a highly unusual dude. If our country ever becomes a monarchy, I could easily see him as king.

A friend of mine recently called my attention to *Pictures at the Revolution* by Marc Harris (Penguin, 2008) in which *The Graduate* is discussed by Mike Nichols and Buck Henry:

> Charles Grodin, a thirty-one-year-old TV and theater performer with a growing list of credits, impressed them both with a very sharp reading. "Grodin got very close," says Nichols. "His reading was hilarious, he's

brilliantly talented, and he understood the jokes. But he didn't look like Benjamin to me."

"Chuck Grodin gave the best reading," says Henry. "And maybe one of the best readings I've ever heard in my career, so funny and interesting. He thinks we offered him the part—I don't think we did. I don't remember his screen test, whereas Dustin's was really memorable."

Dustin Hoffman is a brilliant actor. We were in Lee Strasberg's class together. I have no doubt he gave a memorable screen test. I also have no doubt he had the script well ahead of the night before he did the test.

Sometime in the early sixties, years before all of this, I saw Dustin standing on a street corner near where I lived. He said he was looking for me, because he was directing something in the basement of a church and he wanted me to be in it. There would be no pay, of course. I told him I couldn't, because I had to work (driving a cab at that time). As I walked away, I looked back at him still standing on the corner. I remember thinking to myself, *God, I wonder what's going to happen to him?* Obviously, he's worked so hard and deeply deserves everything that's happened to him. I think he's a magnificent actor.

Mike Nichols wrote me a note after *The Graduate* screen test saying he'd like me to do *Catch-22* with him. That helped, but what really kept *The Graduate* situation from getting to me was a telegram I received soon after the test from Renée Taylor, saying she wanted to meet with me. My friend now of over fifty years, Gene Wilder, got Renée and me together. Through Renée I met her friend Elaine May, which led me to doing *The Heartbreak Kid*, which really launched my movie career.

The French Girl

Right around this time in the late sixties, I was living in an apartment in New York. One day I answered the phone, and there was a French girl on the line. It was a wrong number, but we began to chat. She told me she was a young actress recently arrived from Paris to screen test for the role of a sexy young woman in a movie. She was charming and somewhat flirtatious. After a while, I asked for her number. I was, of course, single. She wouldn't give it to me but took mine and said she'd call again.

About a week later she did, and again we had a flirtatious conversation, and again she wouldn't give me her number but said she'd call again. These weekly calls went on for about a month, until she finally gave me her number. That would prove to be an unconsciously self-destructive move on her part. She said she'd still prefer to call me. I didn't ask why, but I chose to respect her wishes and didn't call her.

After about a half-dozen phone calls, she started to ask me about my dating life. I told her I was seeing a girl, and she began to ask about her. After the second call, when she continued to ask about my new girlfriend, I began to feel suspicious. I wasn't sure what I was suspicious about, just suspicious.

I called my girlfriend and asked her if she had any girlfriends from France. She said she didn't. I then gave her the French girl's number and asked her to look through her phone book to see if that number belonged to anyone she knew. It didn't.

As weeks went by, the French girl continued to call and continued to want to know what the latest was with the girl I was seeing. So I asked my girlfriend to again carefully go through her phone book to see if the girl's number corresponded to any in her book. This time she found it. It didn't belong to a French girl but to a chubby friend of hers who was very good at doing accents.

I asked my friend to put together a small group of people, including the friend who did accents so well, and we'd all go to Central Park and have a picnic. The next Sunday about five of us sat on the side of a hill in Central Park and had our picnic. The chubby girl who was good at accents sat a few feet from me.

The next day the "French girl" called me again to ask me what I had done over the weekend. I told her I'd gone to the park with some friends and had a picnic. She asked me if it was fun. I said, "Well, you were there, what did you think?" There was a long, uncomfortable silence, and she finally said goodbye, without the French accent.

A couple of years went by, of course without any calls from the "French girl." My girlfriend and I had gone our separate ways. She had moved to California. One day the phone rang, and it was the "French girl" using her own voice. She asked me if I had heard from my former girlfriend. I said I hadn't. She then said she had driven off a cliff in California and was dead.

Given my past experience with this girl, I was dubious. Incredibly, she wanted to chat some more about this and that, but I quickly got off the phone and called my former girlfriend's brother. He confirmed she had driven off a cliff and felt it was an accident. But, in fact, she had died. Sheila was in her twenties.

Simon and Garfunkel
and My Politics?

In 1969, I directed a Simon and Garfunkel special for CBS. Because of Paul and Art's prominence, they were given a prime-time slot on Sunday night. My television directing credits at the time were my two firings from *Candid Camera*.

Actually, Paul and Art didn't ask me to direct the special. They asked me to go out and meet with the leading documentarians in the field, which I did. They were all impressive but were talking about something other than what we had in mind. Eventually, I said, "I think I should direct it." Paul and Art said, "Fine."

I'm not sure what the network was expecting—most likely a musical special with maybe one or two guest stars—but Paul and Art were more than open to my idea that we make a documentary special intercutting footage of what was going on in America and in Vietnam that provoked Paul to write some of his songs.

To be upfront with everyone, I sent the network an outline of exactly what the show would be: It would include the Poor People's march on Washington; footage of our three slain leaders, President Kennedy, Robert Kennedy, and Martin Luther King, Jr.; and Robert Kennedy with the migrant workers' leader, César Chávez.

Paul and I traveled to Delano, California, to meet with Mr. Chávez, and our crew followed Paul and Art around the country, filming them in concert. Paul and I attended a union meeting that César Chávez chaired. The discussion was whether they should have a mariachi band or food—they couldn't afford both. Paul arranged it so they could. I have a letter from Mr. Chávez thanking Paul and me for giving him so much of our time. He was an inspiration to me, a role model for helping others in need.

We made the show using the facilities of Robert Drew Associates. Robert Drew was considered by many to be the father of video vérité, meaning documentaries. He had two credits on the special, executive producer and executive in charge of production. He was a self-described Rockefeller Republican—whatever that meant. He had a portrait of Nelson Rockefeller on the wall behind his desk.

Nelson Rockefeller gave us the Rockefeller Drug Laws, which were the harshest in the nation and responsible for ruining thousands of people's lives. More about that later.

Governor Rockefeller, that paragon of virtue, died from having a heart attack while having sex with his mistress.

Anyhow, while I was working on our special, Robert Drew was off in an editing room of his own putting together an entirely different special from our footage: the making of a song or something.

When he saw my "rough assemblage," he called Paul and

Art and me into his office and pronounced it "not airworthy." He then said, "The only way this show can be saved is if Chuck removes himself from control and turns the reins over to me." Paul and Art looked at me for my response—a thirty-four-year-old newcomer challenged by the father of documentaries.

I said, "Bob, you're off in another room making a special none of us have any interest in. I suggest *you* leave the premises and let me complete what I'm doing."

I worked through the night with the editors and took the rough assemblage to its next step: a rough cut. Bob looked at it and said, "That's the best rough cut I've ever seen."

When the special was completed, we waited for the reaction. There was a very loud sound of silence, and then urgent meetings were called.

I was angrily confronted by a representative of the ad agency for the sponsor, AT&T. He said to me, "You're using our money to sell your ideology!" I asked him what he saw as my ideology, and he snapped, "The humanistic approach." I was honestly baffled. I said, "You mean there are people against the humanistic approach?" He said, "You're goddammed right there are!"

What I was too naïve to understand was that in the sixties as well as today, unfortunately, people will almost always put their economic interests over any concern for equal rights, which this special clearly was calling for, and AT&T felt it might offend some of their Southern affiliates. Also, not everyone was necessarily against the war in Vietnam in 1969. As a result, AT&T removed their name from the special after having paid for it.

Right around that time, I was having dinner with some friends at the Russian Tea Room in New York. Sitting nearby was the fellow from the ad agency, and we all heard him say, "Simon and Garfunkel are under the spell of this Svengali figure, Charles Grodin." One of my friends immediately spoke up to let him know I was sitting right there, and any further talk of me or Svengali, for that matter, stopped. The man from the ad agency obviously didn't know Paul Simon or Art Garfunkel, because I've never met anyone with stronger opinions than Paul or Art. The idea that they would be under anyone's spell, mine or even Svengali's, is ludicrous.

I do remember that before AT&T removed their name, the fella from the ad agency had asked for certain changes. One I particularly recall: they were concerned with Coretta Scott King saying, "Poverty is a child without an education." They wanted me to lower the sound on her speaking. I asked to what level? The answer was, "Make it inaudible." (I recently learned that my phone service is with AT&T. I hope they don't read this and make it impossible for me to get a dial tone.)

We made no changes. Next, I was called in to meet with the head of program practices for CBS, or what would be more popularly known as the censor. His name was William Tankersly. We spoke at length, and he and to their great credit CBS decided to let the special run exactly as we had presented it with no changes at all.

The Alberto-Culver Company became the sponsor by simply paying for air costs, as I recall $180,000. They also had the late actor Robert Ryan come on before the special,

Songs of America, began, to say the network felt that Simon and Garfunkel had earned the right to express their opinion.

On the broadcast, the American public heard "Bridge Over Troubled Water" for the first time. It was played over a shot of the train carrying Robert Kennedy's body across the country as people on train platforms stood in silence, saluting or weeping. After that we went to our first commercial break, and one million people switched to another channel.

The special did not get a good rating. The *Washington Post* ran an editorial expressing amazement that the special even got on the air. The Nixon White House requested a copy of it, and my agent suggested I pursue work in some other aspect of show business.

However, the special became a CBS entry in the world-wide Montreux Television Festival, and forty years later the Paley Center for Media, formerly known in New York as the Museum of Television and Radio, is hoping to honor the special, Paul, and Art.

Beginning with that special, I've always been identified with being on the left. The truth is I don't have any politics and actually have more positions that would be considered conservative than liberal.

When I had my cable show, I often spoke about the homeless and people in dire need, or those I felt were being treated unfairly. I also was on television during the impeachment of President Clinton, which I was strongly against, but then it turned out most on the right agreed with me. Recently, I was contacted by a group that wanted me to join them in trying to impeach President Bush. I had no interest in that, either.

People tend to make snap judgments, because they don't have the time or intellectual energy to look further. Once I spoke at an event where one of the other speakers was the late William F. Buckley, Jr. I said I don't measure people by right or left or liberal or conservative but by those who care about others and those who don't. Mr. Buckley let me know he appreciated what I had to say, even though some of his positions, in my opinion, obviously lacked compassion. May he rest in peace, his positions were heartfelt, but that doesn't make him, if you'll pardon the expression, *right.*

I believe everyone should work for a living, but those who are truly unable should not be abandoned by the government. I think we should have much greater punishment for bullies.

I do *not* think drugs should be legalized, and I believe we should have stronger protection and punishment for drinking and driving. I'm against the estate tax. Frankly, I see myself as a compassionate conservative—whatever that or any label means. I have a friend who always identifies himself as a Reagan Republican, but he can't tell me what that means. I don't know, either. The two R's work nicely, though, just as the two C's in compassionate and conservative do.

I am willing to give up certain rights to privacy for more security. On other questions I respond specifically given the circumstances of our times, and I'm not even remotely uncomfortable in saying, "I don't know." That's why I say I have no politics, unless you want to say paying a lot of attention to people in dire need is a political position instead of a human one.

Years ago I became good friends with a New York Mets pitcher who at this writing is part of the New York Yankee broadcasting team, Al Leiter. Recently, a reporter wrote me and said he was doing a story about Al, who may or may not run for political office, and Al suggested he talk to me. The reporter wrote in his letter that Al had told him, "Even though Chuck and I are on opposite ends of the political spectrum, we're friends."

I called Al and asked him what made him think we were on opposite ends of the political spectrum? Al then asked me a series of questions. One was, "How do you feel about all this f this and f that?" He seemed surprised that I was as much against it as he was. He then asked me a number of other political questions and was startled to learn that our opinions were almost identical. Al knew that for years I was hanging out with a very famous liberal, so he assumed I was one, too. I told him my friend and I were always in a constant debate.

You really don't know who anyone is or what they feel unless you ask them specific questions or live with them.

Benefactors

Of course, my first benefactor was Eleni Kiamos, my classmate at Uta Hagen's who as I've said introduced me to a woman friend who put me in a lead in a off-off-Broadway show, which led to my getting an agent. Eleni then introduced me to Lee Strasberg, then to a casting director, which led to my starting to work in television. It's only all these years later that I realize how much Eleni did for me when I was beginning, when you really need a benefactor. I always adored her without fully grasping how many doors she opened for me.

Then, of course, there's Gene Wilder, who put Renée Taylor in touch with me, which led to my meeting Elaine May. I always considered Gene a major benefactor of mine.

I first met Elaine May at Gene Wilder's apartment. She walked over to me and said, "Gene says wonderful things about you." In a misguided effort to amuse, I said, "Boy, you're really coming on." She looked at me as though she had no idea what was happening. When she left, I gave her my coat, because I thought she'd be cold outside. Talk about a confusing encounter.

In a later meeting, Renée Taylor and Joe Bologna asked me if I would mind if Elaine May came to see *Lovers and Other Strangers*, which I directed when it was previewing on Broadway. I said, "I'd love to hear anything she says." All I remember about that meeting is Elaine prefacing every observation with something like, "I'm sure Chuck has already thought of this."

A couple of years later I was directing Renée and Joe in a piece they had written for Public Broadcasting. It was a scene with a couple in bed. Halfway through rehearsal I said to Joe, "You should be directing this (Joe was a director), and I should be playing your part." Joe said, "Well, we based the character on you."

I climbed into bed. Joe took my seat in the director's chair. Elaine May saw the piece and told me she was being asked to direct movies, and she was going to put me in the next one that came along that was right for me. That was *The Heartbreak Kid*, which a lot of major stars wanted to do, but she said she wanted Charles Grodin. Most people in show business had never heard of me at that time.

Elaine then persuaded Warren Beatty to put me in *Heaven Can Wait*. I then did *Ishtar* with her. I believe that movie may be too hip for a lot of rooms. People familiar with the nightclub circuit might be very surprised by who's on-stage at times. I got excellent reviews in *Ishtar*, and that had something to do with my being cast in *Midnight Run*.

I've known Elaine May for over forty years, and since that first meeting I've never had one uncomfortable moment with her. As I've said, she's always been my biggest supporter in show business. She was once quoted as saying about herself, "I'm not warm, but I'm polite." Around me she's warm as well as polite. As a director, she never criticizes. She'll suggest something else.

Of course, I love Elaine May.

Once, in the 1960s, I was delivering a handwritten script (which is how I still write) to Studio Duplicating, a typing service on West Forty-fourth Street in Manhattan. I can still hear George, the nice man who always answered the phone, "Hello, Studio."

One day when I delivered my latest longhand script to be typed, he said for reasons still not entirely clear to me, "Do you know Herb Gardner?" I later learned that Herb Gardner delivered his scripts printed in longhand. I, at least, wrote in what is known as script. There were probably other reasons why George asked, "Do you know Herb Gardner?" He was prescient, because circumstances or fate got Herb Gardner and me to meet about a year later, and I've never had a closer friend than Herb.

Before I met Herb, I had heard him on the great Jean Shepherd's radio show. Herb presented himself as the PR man for the Atlantic Ocean. "We're deeper. We have more fish."

My first interaction with him came when Elaine May told him to get me for a role in his play *The Goodbye People*, which they were going to do in Stockbridge, Massachusetts. My girlfriend at the time was going to be in it, and I would be there anyway.

I told him I didn't know how to play a character who

says whole sentences while he's sleeping. Looking back, I'm amazed he didn't persist, because as I later discovered he was known to be endlessly persevering. I didn't do the play, but we instantly became friends. The brilliant Bob Dishy played the part, and he pulled it off beautifully.

Herb taught me so much by what many saw as his "odd behavior" and I saw as artistic courage in action. In many ways he became a role model to me, and I know to many others—not only by what he wrote, but by who he was.

Herb died in 2003. He had been in the process of dying for several years, no doubt because of his lifelong habit of always having a cigarette in his mouth or at least in his hand. One of my biggest regrets in life is that I not only didn't say anything to him about smoking, I apparently didn't even notice sufficiently. There was so much about him that would keep you from noticing the cigarette. He was as compelling a personality as I've ever met. He wrote *A Thousand Clowns* when he was in his twenties. If you choose to read it, you won't be sorry.

A good example of Herb's integrity came during a period when he was getting many offers to turn *A Thousand Clowns* into a television series. He really could have used the money but he declined, saying, "Because I wouldn't be able to oversee the quality of each segment."

I worked with Herb in 1974. His play *Thieves* had opened in New Haven and Boston and gotten bad reviews. Marlo Thomas called me in California where I was making movies and asked if I would come to Boston to take a look at it. She was considering going in and replacing the lead actress.

I flew to Boston and watched the play, with Marlo sitting next to me taking a quick look at me every minute or so to see my reaction. Herb and Marlo and I met afterward and I said, "I don't know how good I can make it, but I can make it better than this." That was enough for Marlo to step into the leading role.

One evening after a performance, Herb and I sat in the back of the theater and two women walked up the aisle, saw us, and snickered in disdain. "They're trying to fix it!" The producers left the play, as well as the director. I became the director and the producer along with my friend from all those years ago in summer stock, Richard Scanga, who actually had experience as a producer, which I didn't have. I began to work with Herb on the script. I asked him to cut certain passages I felt didn't work, and he refused even though the play hadn't gotten good notices. Herb simply said, "I'd rather close it than cut those sentences." Instead of that attitude alienating me, it intrigued me. He did agree with me on enough changes that the play opened in New York, and despite getting mixed notices, it became the longest-running play in New York that season. The run, of course, had a lot to do with Marlo's ability to draw a crowd.

Among the many things that Herb did for me over the years was to suggest me for *Same Time, Next Year*. He also gave me the idea for my play *The Price of Fame*. He introduced me to many people I probably never would have met. I became friends with Paddy Chayefsky, Jules Feiffer, Shel Silverstein, Dick Schaap, Jule Styne, Jimmy Breslin, Elaine Stritch, and Bob Fosse.

One night at a gathering at Herb's apartment, Bob Fosse started to tease me about my plan to open on Broadway in a two-character play, *Same Time, Next Year*. He said, "With two characters they're going to have to love everything you do. They're going to have to love the way you sit, the way you stand, the way you walk." That was Fosse's sense of fun, which frankly I enjoyed.

Herb stepped in to stop him from talking to me that way, but then I said to Fosse, "Well, in the movie of [and I named a movie he directed], you had lots and lots of people, and *that* wasn't successful." Although we traded insults, Bob Fosse and I really liked each other. I once took a very glamorous movie star who was *only* a friend of mine to a party at his apartment. He took one look at her and was immediately smitten and made his move. Then feeling guilty—believing she was my girlfriend—he went to another room and gave me a CD of the original score of *Evita* before it opened on Broadway. He and my movie star pal shared great times together.

Later in my relationship with Herb, he and his wife, Barbara, took me aside and told me they felt I was dominating their dinner parties too much, which is definitely a flaw of mine. Instead of retorting by saying, "Well, *you* . . . ," I accepted their valid criticism, simply because I agreed with them. If somebody's not on, I will jump in and take over, in hindsight even in *my* opinion inappropriately.

On the other hand, at some gatherings after that when there would be a lull, people would look at me, but I *didn't* jump in. Over the years I listened to other criticisms from Herb, some of which I didn't agree with, but I chose not to rebut him because I knew he was coming from a place of genuine love for me. Here's an example of what I mean. It's a quote that he gave me for my first book, *It Would Be So Nice If You Weren't Here.*

One of Grodin's best performances: bringing to his writing the same insightful humor and persuasive humanity that he brings to his acting, he has come up with a kind of intrepid explorer's guidebook through that most treacherous of terrains—the dark valleys and paper mountains of show business. Like the best of Grodin's comic roles, it's about the survival of all of us who believe we are sane in a world gone mad, a world we need to be part of that seems to need no part of us. When you finish this book, I think you'll be glad as I am that Grodin *is*, in fact, and will remain, here.

I'll always cherish Herb Gardner, even if he had chosen not *to give me a quote.*

Herb once went to a screening of a movie I had written and coproduced. Afterward he was barely speaking to me because he felt I had cut so much out of my original script, which he loved. We got back on track after I explained to him that we had originally screened it with all that I had written still in it, and it just didn't play as well. At that screening with about a thousand people in the audience, there was only one person consistently laughing out loud—Elaine May.

Steambath

When I was making the movie *Catch-22*, in 1969 and 1970, I became good friends with Anthony Perkins, who was a good friend of Orson Welles, who was also in the cast. Tony introduced me to Orson as someone he would enjoy knowing. Something in the way Tony described me suggested I was a good storyteller, the last thing Orson was interested in having around, because Orson was the storyteller. Orson looked at me like I was a lamp whose light he would like to turn off.

He also chose to tell Mike Nichols what to do with the cameras whenever he was in a scene, and wasn't a bit self-conscious about it.

At some point, a friend from New York who was coproducing a play called to discuss suggestions I might have for directors. I knew Tony Perkins was interested in directing, and even though he had never directed, I thought he could because he was so bright and gifted, so I suggested him. He ended up getting the job.

The play was *Steambath* by Bruce Jay Friedman, a brilliant comedy playwright and novelist. The star was comedian Dick Shawn. During rehearsals, Dick was fired, and Rip Torn took over. Not too long after that, still in rehearsal, Rip was fired, and they asked me to take over. By that time rehearsals had gone on so long, Tony was in Hollywood keeping a prior movie commitment. A director named Jacques Levy took over. After a couple of weeks, preview audiences started to come, and the play and I were being received extremely well. Then they fired me.

The reasoning was the play was working well, but to recoup all the long rehearsal expenses, it would be good to get a name, and they did—Tony Perkins.

Tony came in. The play opened and wasn't successful. The feeling was Tony was miscast. The immediate ramification of this for me was it ended my relationship with Tony. You don't replace a friend in something where he suggested you as the director.

I wasn't aware of the impact this firing had on me until I started having dreams about being replaced. This was a first—being fired at the thing I was the best at.

True to my rebounding nature, a short time later I wrote a play about someone fearing he's going to be fired as the director. Alan Arkin starred in it in 1971 in Nyack, New York. *One of the All-Time Greats* opened off-Broadway in 1992, got an excellent review from the *Times*, and had a successful run.

The paths of Bruce J. Friedman, the writer of *Steambath*, and mine crossed years later, after I became known in the movies. He told me that his sons had told him not to fire me, because I was the reason the play was suddenly working. It always had the brilliant Hector Elizondo in it, but my role was the lead, the protagonist.

About a year after I was fired, Bruce went to the office of my friend, who was *Steambath*'s coproducer, and said, "Guess who's playing the lead in *The Heartbreak Kid*?" My friend said, "I know."

Ironically, the short story on which *The Heartbreak Kid* is based was written by Bruce J. Friedman.

Appearing on Johnny Carson and David Letterman to Show the Real Me?

In the early seventies, while appearing as a guest with Johnny Carson on the *Tonight Show*, I presented myself as a malcontent, a kind of person bothered by everything. I did this because I felt if I just came out and said how I was excited about my new movie or maybe told some anecdote about it, it really wouldn't be sufficient for someone to stay up late to watch, so I made up a character who was always outraged by this or that.

To this day, decades later, I still play the malcontent with David Letterman. I entered recently in an agitated state, claiming the stage manager had said to me just before I came on, "Your jacket won't televise well." Of course, no such thing happened.

When I began to do this all those years ago with Johnny, people would sometimes genuinely be offended by my responses. Johnny would ask me how I was, and I'd say, "I don't want to answer that, because I know you're not really interested in the answer," and the audience would hiss, and they meant it, too! Of course, they would have no way of knowing that I was under exclusive contract to Johnny Carson as a guest.

I was originally interested in going on Johnny Carson's show in 1973 to show those people who might have seen me in *The Heartbreak Kid*, in which I left my wife on our honeymoon, that I wasn't really a cad. Many would say that the persona I felt had to choose was worse than caddish. Over the years, I continued to play often unsympathetic roles in movies. The doctor who unwittingly turns Rosemary over to the bad guys in *Rosemary's Baby* came prior to *The Heartbreak Kid*. To this day, amazingly to me, some people confront me over that dastardly deed. I've actually gotten into polite debates justifying Doctor Hill's actions.

I followed *Rosemary's Baby* with *Catch-22*, where I threw a prostitute out the window. When Alan Arkin confronted me in the movie on that, I explained, "A lot of people are killed during wartime."

After I did the movie *The Incredible Shrinking Woman*, my mother said more than one of her friends had seriously asked her why I hadn't helped my tiny wife clear up the mess after she dropped a number of dishes. In the movie, the camera cuts to a shot of me ruefully shaking my head in the breakfast nook, but not getting up to help.

I explained to my mother that they couldn't actually shrink Lily. They just made everything around her superlarge, and if I had run in to help, I would have appeared tiny as well, and that wasn't the story. Besides, I said I wasn't even there on the day they shot Lily dropping the dishes. My mother advised me to forget about it: "No one will know what you're talking about."

Years later, with David Letterman, we devised a bit where I came out but he wasn't there behind the desk. He was actually in his office, but he said on the phone, which the audience could hear, that he was at home. He had an appointment with the cable people, who were late. I said in an exasperated tone that was really inappropriate, "If you are hosting a show, you can't let a cable appointment take precedence." After my appearance a lot of letters came in saying I should have been more understanding of David's situation.

When I began my cable show, Johnny had recently re-tired. He wrote and asked if I'd like to have dinner with him whenever I was in California. One night I went to a restaurant and joined Johnny and his wife. As I began to talk about my cable show, he was openly bored. I found his response funny. I challenged him by asking what he thought was interesting. He then began to describe an upcoming event in astronomy. I looked at him and said, "You find that more interesting than show business?" He did. At the end of the dinner, he asked if I would like to join him on a sa-fari in Africa. I said, "What! Sleep in a tent with you while wild animals try to get at us?" I chose not to go. Another mistake.

When Johnny passed away, I was so sorry to hear that he had been alone, no longer with his wife. It's always sad to me that someone who brought so much enjoyment to all of us spent a substantial part of his life in unhappiness.

I have some notes from Johnny I'd like to share with you. I have no memory of what prompted the following note, but it's the only one of its kind I've ever received from a man—or woman for that matter.

I had received three residual checks for my appearances on the *Best of Carson* DVDs. They totaled eight dollars and change. I wrote Johnny that I always felt that I was a tiny part of the success of the *Tonight Show*, I just hadn't realized *how* tiny.

April 4 '97

Dear Chuck,

I apologize for our errant bookkeeping at the Carson Company — and will correct the over payment by withholding the appropriate amount in future checks.

Thank you for calling this to our attention.

love
JC.

Johnny had bypass surgery, and I wondered if this was in store in the future for me as a talk show host, so I asked him to get me some figures on costs. Ironically, sometime after this letter both Regis Philbin and David Letterman had bypass surgery. I haven't had that issue, but if I ever do, I'll certainly study Johnny's research.

> JOHNNY CARSON
>
> 5/1/99
>
> Dear Chvcic,
> As per your suggestion, I've checked around for the best price on Bi-pass surgery. The low bidder was St. Olaf's in Bemidji, Minn.
> double Bi-pass - $1550
> gradruple - slightly higher at 1400 - But they throw in a vasectomy and one months' free icefishing on Lake Hiawatha.
>   Your obediant
>   Servant
>   J. Carson

I also have some notes from David Letterman, but I don't think it's appropriate to publish them until at *least* both of us are dead.

Memorable Encounters
with Icons

My encounters with the following icons were relatively brief but for me unforgettable and inform my behavior.

In the midseventies I once had lunch with the great English actor Trevor Howard at his house outside of London. We were sitting in his garden. At one point he asked, "Is your driver out there in the car?" I said yes. He said, "Have him come in and join us." He did. When I left London I gave my driver some money in an envelope. He said, "There could be nothing in this envelope, and I still consider it a privilege to have driven you." I believe the lunch with Trevor Howard had something to do with his feelings.

Especially memorable was the time I was working with Sir John Gielgud. I was going to see the previous day's filming and asked if he'd like to join me. When we got to the screening room, he called out to the director, "I hope it's all right I'm here. Chuck asked me to come." Of course, it was. Sir John Gielgud's modesty was wonderful to see.

Another time I went to a reception after a screening of *The Heartbreak Kid*, the first movie where I played a leading role. Groucho Marx was there, and I was taken over to meet him. He looked at me and said, "Hated the movie, loved my seat."

The Unexpected

In 1974, I was asked to do a two-character play on Broadway called *Same Time, Next Year*. The female lead was to be played by Ellen Burstyn. We had never met, so the producer felt it was essential we get together just to make sure we got along.

Ellen drove into New York from her house in Snedens Landing, picked me up, and drove us back to her place. I noticed she wore little or no makeup and was beautiful.

We spent several hours at her house talking about the play and from the very beginning liked each other very much.

I had arranged for a car to come get me and take me back to the city. As I got up to leave, Ellen said, "I have to tell you something. I have an ex-husband, Neil, who overdosed on LSD. It's had a permanent effect on him. At one point he called himself Neil Nephew. He's confined in an institution, but he periodically manages to escape and seeks me out as well as any man I have anything to do with personally or professionally. I'm terribly sorry to lay this on you."

For a moment, I was speechless, then managed to say as casually as I could, "Oh, I wouldn't worry about that."

Of course, just the opposite was true. Of all the things I've ever done, acting requires by far the greatest concentration as well as relaxation, and the idea that my costar's ex-husband might escape from an institution and appear at any time and do God knows what wasn't exactly what I had in mind as an aid for my concentration or relaxation.

Nevertheless, I continued to reassure Ellen not to worry one moment about it.

As soon as I got back to my apartment I called the producer who, if memory serves, already knew about this. I asked that a meeting be called to discuss how to deal with the situation. I asked Herb Gardner to be my representative at the meeting, as I was going to try to think about this as little as possible. It was decided that there would be guards at the theater to keep an eye out and a photo of Neil discreetly placed in the box office.

I guess no one thought much about the rehearsal period, because a week in, Ellen looked past me and said, "Oh, it's Neil." I turned and saw an average-looking fella staring at us. Ellen walked over to him. I went over, sat down in a chair, and looked the other way. I don't remember if we resumed rehearsals that day, but soon we moved on as though it hadn't happened. I asked no questions, and no one spoke about it to me.

Sometime a few weeks into rehearsal the extremely experienced director said that the new-to-Broadway playwright told him he would just as soon not open the play out of town in Boston if this was what it was going to look like. In other words, he was suggesting we consider closing the play in rehearsal. I said, "This isn't what we're going to do in front of an audience. We're figuring out the roles." Ellen Bursytn and I had to play our characters five years older in each of the six scenes—not a job for your boy or girl next door.

The play was a smash in Boston. There was an unusual moment during the run there. One day, from across the large lobby of the hotel where we were staying, the late Van Johnson, a great movie star, called out to me, "You work *so* hard." My dad would have been proud.

Same Time, Next Year was a standing room only hit in New York, with lines around the block. Lucille Ball came backstage to say hello to me, sat down at the makeup table, freshened up her makeup, and without turning around said to me, "We should work together sometime." When Bob Hope came, they could only find a seat for him in the balcony. I had an earlier experience with Bob Hope.

One time early in my experience with Johnny Carson, I evidently went so far that the executive producer, Fred De Cordova, said to my friend the talent coordinator, "We won't be seeing Mr. Grodin for a while." After Johnny's monologue hadn't been received as it normally was, I had come out as the first guest and said, "Rather than me trying to be funny in this atmosphere, why don't we run a clip from an earlier appearance where I was." Before they banned me, they received an appreciative call from Bob Hope wanting to know, "Who is that kid?"

Ellen won a Tony Award for her performance in *Same Time, Next Year*, and we both won an Outer Critics Circle Award.

This naïveté that was expressed by the playwright of *Same Time, Next Year* when he suggested we should possibly close the play in rehearsal manifested itself from when the producer Ray Stark called me after the first reading of *Seems Like Old Times* with Goldie Hawn, Chevy Chase, and me to ask, "What are we going to do about Chevy?" I said, "What do you mean?" He said, "He's ad-libbing all over the place." I said, "Ask him not to." They did, so he didn't, and was incredibly charming in the role.

It happened again after the first reading of *The Heartbreak Kid* when they discussed replacing me, because I had begun "working on the part" instead of performing it as I'd done in the screen test. Elaine May reminded them they'd already seen me perform it.

My point in saying all this is it's shocking how many people in positions of real authority, right up to the president, of course, sometimes absolutely don't know what they're talking about. That's why all the rejection I've dealt with never affected me in the way you might think. I don't accept that the rejecter knows what he or she is talking about.

For example, when one of my plays is rejected, that's meaningless to me as far as its value is concerned, because someone who's *reading* it rejected it, but I've already seen it *performed* in front of a highly appreciative audience. Otherwise, I wouldn't have sent it to anyone.

Recently, I gave a Broadway producer a play of mine that has four stars committed to playing the four roles. I explained I'd seen it read several times to large audiences and that it had received an outstanding response. The producer read it and was completely dismissive of it. It didn't get me down because I felt I was dealing with a fool. Gene Wilder said, "With you writing it and those names connected to it . . . ," and then he just shook his head.

Over the years, especially in movies, I've offered a lot of ideas—script changes and so forth. There are exceptions, of course. Neil Simon's *Seems Like Old Times* quickly comes to mind. Not only would someone come over to you if you left a "the" out, but once in a scene where Robert Guillaume was playing the piano I was standing behind him tapping my fingers on his shoulders and was told to please don't do that. I've never experienced the control that was exercised over that movie. In fairness, it was a big hit, but I believe you limit me and others with that strong a controlling hand over my hand's tapping. I mean, c'mon . . .

On many films, I let the director know that I may offer a lot of ideas, and I quickly add that if they aren't embraced, my disposition will be the same as if they were. As a producer, director, or writer, I would welcome any actor's suggestions with the understanding that if they weren't accepted, "no sulking allowed." I never sulk or pout as I've seen others do when they don't get their way; it can put a dark cloud over everything.

I had a lot of thoughts about *Same Time, Next Year* that I shared with the playwright and the director, and they were used. As I've said, if they weren't I would have gone right ahead in good spirits with the script that I signed on to do.

It wasn't evident to me how much the playwright's wife, and I assume the playwright, resented all of this, since my ideas were accepted without any discord, and the play was a smash. That's why I was very surprised at what happened at a party after I had left the play—which, by the way, angered the producer, even though I had fulfilled my contract of staying with it for seven months after the Broadway opening. The producer assumed I had a big money offer to do a movie, but I didn't. I just felt that with rehearsal and the out of town try-out and previews, it had been almost ten months, and it was enough. To make matters worse from the producer's point of view, when I chose to leave, Ellen Burstyn did as well.

Anyway, the playwright's wife was at this party, and I asked if her husband would be joining us. She stared at me and said he was meeting with someone he hoped to get to play my part in the movie. The play had been sold to the movies for a million dollars. That was how I heard I wouldn't be asked to play the role. The playwright's wife seemed to thoroughly enjoy giving me the news. Not wanting to give her any satisfaction, I casually asked, "Oh, who's directing?" And she, to rub it in, said, "Oh, if we get this actor, *anyone* would direct it."

The director of the play, the brilliant Gene Saks, wasn't asked to direct the movie, even though he had directed several hit movies, so maybe they had a beef with Gene *and* me, which is really ironic, because the play of *Same Time, Next Year* was the hit of the writer's life in the theater.

Ellen Burstyn, who played her role in the movie, has always given me a lot of credit for the success of the play, but evidently the playwright and his wife saw it differently. In fairness, I'm sure their feelings are as genuine as mine, but I wish that the playwright had at least made me aware of them when we were working together.

I was recently telling my friend John Gabriel, as insightful a man as I've ever met, the story about the playwright and his wife, and he said something quite startling to me, which I now believe. He said, "They weren't upset with you about your input. How could they be upset with you for helping hand them their biggest hit?"

He said that, like the producer, they were upset with me because I was leaving their standing room only hit, no doubt shortening the run and costing them money. It ran a total of three years, but I guess they felt if Ellen Burstyn and I had stayed longer, it might have run five years. I don't believe they were angry at Ellen, because they knew she left only because I did.

That never occurred to me, but John is probably right, because the producer was so angry we were leaving he refused to throw a party for Ellen and me, so we threw it and invited him. He came, too, and had a good time!

Until John Gabriel said that to me, it had never occurred to me in more than thirty years, even though there was a pretty obvious clue in the producer's attitude. What I take from that is *even though you're positive you understand something, you may be dead wrong!* Politicians, beware! Of course, if John *is* right, then the playwright's wife's hostile behavior toward me seems *more* offensive.

A few performances before the opening night of *Same Time, Next Year*, in the middle of a scene, a voice called out from the balcony to me saying, "I like your robe." Security guards removed Ellen's former husband Neil from the theater. Needless to say, the rest of that performance was not up to our usual level.

I later learned that Neil committed suicide by jumping out of a window. So many people tragically have no idea what drugs can do to them, even though it's in the news every day that people are dying from drug abuse.

The year after the play I did the movie *Heaven Can Wait*, which I believe is as good a movie as I've ever been involved with, mostly because of the stunning performances of Warren Beatty and Julie Christie.

My first connection to Julie Christie was when I overheard her talking on the phone in the Palo Alto, California, mansion we were filming in. I heard her say some nice things about me, and since I was available, as evidently she was, that was enough for me to ask her out. She had gone with Warren years earlier. Julie Christie and I sat in a restaurant, and she said, "I have no idea what I'm doing here with you, I have all these houseguests." I honestly can't remember what I said to that, but at least she didn't walk out on dinner. A few days later she invited me to a pool party at the house she had taken for the filming. I was the only male there, and Julie and all the women were walking around bare-breasted. At one point, Julie came over to me and said, "Don't be bothered by this." I said, "I'm not bothered." Frankly, the writer in me was trying to figure out why they invited me. I wasn't able to—still can't.

That's all I remember about Julie on location. After the picture I was sitting with Warren in some club on the Sunset

Strip and Julie came by and suggested we join her and a friend to go somewhere, but we stayed where we were.

In my experience, Warren Beatty is one of the sweetest, most appealing, and most gifted people I've ever met. My closest female friend of almost forty years, Ria Berkus, and I once followed Warren in his car as he took us to the Playboy mansion, where we'd never been. Warren went to the call box and seemed to be waiting a little longer than you would expect for the gates to open. Ria, who is the single funniest woman I've ever met, said, as though she were speaking from the mansion to the call box, "Sorry, Warren, you've had your share of girls for the month."

Warren's legendary success with women leads me to believe he knew how to talk to girls while the rest of us were still being toilet trained. I believe Warren realized before most of us, if we ever did, that some women are as interested in sex as we men are. That *never* occurred to me.

A Most Formidable
Woman
—or Something

For a time in the seventies I was going out with one of the most formidable women I ever knew. She has achieved quite a lot in her life in areas beyond acting and is known all over the world for her strong feelings about many things. The first time I asked her out she said, "I'll go out with you, but do something dazzling." *Dazzling*, I thought. Right. Yeah. Good luck!

The best I could come up with was to take her to dinner at a really out-of-the-way place that had been around for hundreds of years. I felt she would be impressed by that, and she was. I remember she ordered a Manhattan, which impressed *me*. Afterward I took her to meet some friends of mine she had worked with, who were also very accomplished. I felt she would be impressed that these were my friends. She was. I don't remember impressing her much after that, but we continued to go out. I could make her laugh, and that seemed to get me a lot of points, but most of the time she wasn't laughing but debating me on . . . well, you name it.

She very much liked to go to the theater, and I didn't.

There was one particular play she wanted to see that I had been told by friends would drive me screaming into the night with boredom. Not to say it wasn't any good; I'm sure it was, but let's just say it wasn't my cup of tea. She said, "If you don't like it, we'll leave at intermission." I said, "Really?" She said, "Absolutely." We went to see it. It was everything I thought it would be, which meant I wanted to leave at intermission. She then said, "We can't leave. People from the cast know we're here." I looked at her for a long moment and reminded her of our deal. She again said, "People know we're here." I stayed.

After the play, as we walked up Broadway, we debated what had happened. We were going to meet some friends of mine, and one of them was an official with Amnesty International, an organization that looks into human rights violations. Not that sitting in a theater past the point where you want to leave would in any way be considered a human rights violation, but I thought presenting our cases to an Amnesty official might inject some much needed humor into our latest debate. When we got to my friend's apartment, I said we'd had a disagreement and wanted to present the story for her judgment.

At that point my girlfriend piped up and said she was agreeable to this, if she could be the one to describe what happened. Not the *first* one to describe, the *only* one! In other words, I would get to say nothing. My Amnesty friend gently said that didn't seem quite right. I honestly don't remember what happened after that.

She liked to refer to me, I think affectionately, as having

"exotic neuroses." I don't remember her ever acknowledging that she wasn't exactly the girl next door. We eventually went our separate ways, but whenever I run into her over the years, we always have some laughs. Of course, we chat for only a few minutes.

Some relationships just work better that way.

It must be obvious by now that in some of these stories I name names and in others I don't. Some people deserve to be named, and others deserve the respect of not having that happen.

The All Knowing

I was going out to dinner with a friend of mine in the late 1970s, and I couldn't help but notice he seemed more muscular. I asked him about it, and he said he had run into a guy at a gym who was a trainer, and the fella was training him. He gave me his name, and the trainer started to come to my apartment to train me. While I had been reasonably athletic as a teenager, that was quite a while ago, and I hadn't worked out for years, if ever.

This guy jumped right in and started to work me as though I had told him I'd decided to go for the decathlon. I figured he must know what he's doing (a notion I've long since gotten over about people in all fields), so I went along, even though I couldn't help but notice that after the hour with him, I would just stare vacantly into space for about twenty minutes, having no desire to even consider standing up.

This went on for a couple of months. This is a good lesson learned about the importance of being skeptical, which, given my penchant for questions, I'm amazed didn't inform my judgment when I was forty-five years old!

Eventually, I was so messed up, I couldn't even stand

up to get out of bed. I called the trainer and told him what had happened. He suggested he still come over to "tone me up." I'm still not quite sure how you tone up someone who can't move, but I just let it go and thanked him for everything. I always try to be nice, even in circumstances when logic doesn't call for nice. It felt like it never for one moment occurred to this *all knowing* trainer that he had been very damaging.

My next call was to a doctor who suggested I come see him. I said, "I can't move." He said, "Have an ambulance bring you over." I said, in a nice way, of course, "Thanks, but no thanks." Another character who doesn't see how all knowingly nuts he is.

I found a doctor who suggested that the ambulance bring me to a prominent New York hospital. The next day they wheeled me down the hall. Through my drugged haze (I had gotten myself prescription painkillers because I was in a lot of pain even lying still.) I asked where we were going. A nurse said, "The doctor has scheduled a myelogram for you."

That's a procedure where they inject you with a dye to see exactly where on your spine they're operating. Someone once told me that dye can give you a headache for about twenty years. I had no way of confirming that, but I looked up at the nurses through my haze and said, "I haven't agreed to surgery." The nurses gave me a strange look and wheeled me back to my room.

The doctor, a very nice guy, came to my room and kindly said, "I understand you don't feel you'll need surgery." I said,

"Since I've been in the hospital, I feel the pressure on my lower back has let up a bit, as I'm in a different position than I was at home, as well as now being in traction." I think he already thought I was nuts, so I chose not to tell him I had played a doctor in the movie *Rosemary's Baby*, and even though I played a gynecologist, I felt I knew a little something about backs. Most of the time when I do jokes like that, people think I'm serious.

He took a position at the foot of the bed, bent my leg, and slowly moved it toward my chest. I remember how his eyes widened as he bent it way more than he thought he could, before I asked him to stop.

He then graciously said, "Well, I'm always willing to learn," and it was decided to give bed rest and traction a try. As the days went on, I still wouldn't even attempt to stand, but I felt I was improving.

I asked the night nurse if my girlfriend could visit me after work, which would be around seven p.m. She said that was past visiting hours. I felt that since I had a private room I should be allowed to have a visitor. She glared at me and suggested I could take it up with her supervisor. I did, and the supervisor said that would be fine.

Now I had an enemy in the night nurse, who always acted as though she owned the hospital—all knowing with a chip on her shoulder, and she made no effort to conceal her feelings. I remember trying jokes with her like, "I don't want an enemy giving me a enema." She didn't think anything I said was even remotely funny. I was supposed to rest and relax there for three weeks, but because of the tension with the night nurse, I chose to have an ambulance take me back to my apartment.

My nice doctor offered to move me to a room at the other end of the floor, but I declined. I didn't want to think about that nurse showing up in my new room and confronting me while I was lying flat out. That wouldn't have been a good idea for me or for her. She should have been fired.

Herb Gardner came to the hospital to accompany me in the back of the ambulance, where he and a guy in a white uniform chatted. Herb, I'm sure trying to amuse me, asked the ambulance attendant to share different code descriptions of patients in ambulances. I remember LRGDNR, which means last rights given, do not resuscitate, and LOB, liquor on breath, which also didn't apply to me, which I would have found funny if I hadn't been in pain from the ambulance hitting bumps in the road. Back home, with a lot of help from my girlfriend and two former girlfriends, each doing eight-hour shifts, I was up and around in about a month.

Today I have no back problems at all, but I do have problems with trainers or anyone else who thinks they know everything and with hospital personnel who are hostile to people who can't stand up, or even those who can.

Actually, as I've said, I have a lot of problems with know-it-alls on any subject and *a lot* of problems with anyone expressing hostility in or out of hospitals.

Too many people everywhere foolishly consider themselves authorities. Many years ago I had a meeting with a top executive at a talent agency that represented me. I wasn't working all that much. With full certainty he said, "If you don't make it by the time you're thirty, forget it." I chose not to tell him I was thirty-two. Early in their careers, Clint Eastwood and Burt Reynolds were both dropped by Universal Studios, Burt because they said he couldn't act, and Clint because they said his Adam's apple was too big, and then of course there was the talent executive's report on Fred Astaire, which read, "Can't act, can't sing, can dance a little."

Of course, I'd have to include in this category the executive producer of the Simon and Garfunkel special who pronounced it "not air worthy," and then the next day "the best rough cut I've ever seen."

I've never heard anyone more all knowing than Dr. Laura Schlesinger on the radio. There almost never seems to be any doubt that what she's saying could possibly be anything less than 100 percent right. Even though she only talks to people for a relatively brief period of time, she and, of course, others are more than willing to tell them what to do about something that could impact the rest of their life. Leave your husband, leave your wife questions? No problem, here's what you should do.

It doesn't seem to ever occur to these psychologists that the picture they're getting may not be the full truth. Most people describing a problem can't get the full truth out in five minutes, if we are *ever* capable of seeing it.

Dr. Laura once made a lot of working mothers furious by suggesting they couldn't possibly work regularly and be Dr. Laura's concept of the right kind of mother. Oh, she tells us it can be done if mother and father take off from their jobs and share the responsibility for their children. That comes under the heading of "nice work if you can get it." Dr. Laura, of course, controls where she works, so she can properly look after her children. For me personally looking back as a kid, I don't think I'd much want someone around who seems to know everything about everything, and if I did have someone like that, I sure wouldn't want them around *all* the time.

There doesn't seem to be anything these people don't know. I once heard Dr. Laura tell a caller that "when most people do sit-ups, they really work their hip muscles instead of their stomach muscles." Perish the thought.

Somebody should call and ask, "What do you do if you live with someone who acts as though they know everything about everything?" That's an answer I'd like to hear.

I drove by a sign on a preschool the other day that said it was for children 2.6 to 6 years of age—2.6! It reminded me of a story I heard years ago from some friends who were trying to get their child into a preschool. The little girl was rejected because the instructor said her hand-eye coordination wasn't where it needed to be, and it wouldn't be fair to the child to put her in with a group of kids with superior hand-eye coordination.

When my friends asked how the instructor knew this about their child, he showed them a drawing she was asked to do of a kangaroo. It didn't look much like a kangaroo, but when my friends asked to see the other children's drawings of kangaroos, they didn't look much like kangaroos, either. Their child later became one of the top female athletes in the state.

In preschools, and just about everywhere else in life, don't believe everything you hear.

Part of the know-it-all epidemic is the instant e-mail voting on cable television. A question that was raised recently was, "What countries do you feel should help in Liberia?" Who's doing all this voting? Are they experts on Liberia, or just on Africa in general?

An earlier one was, "What do you think we should do about nuclear weapons in North Korea?" These are questions that the most informed experts wrestle with daily, and yet thousands of people instantly vote on this, and the results are given as though they tell us something.

There are an awful lot of people out there who are willing to give you their opinion on *anything*, whether they know much about the subject or not, so obviously be skeptical, but—forgive me for digressing a moment—*accept all compliments.*

In the 1970s, I was filming a movie in London. We were on location, shooting outside the campus at Oxford University. One night I went to dinner at a restaurant by myself. I sat at a small table for two and faced the wall. To my right and left were the same size tables, only about a foot away from mine. To my right there was a middle-aged couple, the man facing the wall as I was. To my left there was a mother and her daughter in her twenties.

I ordered some kind of meat dish. When I tasted it, it was inedible—filled with fat and startlingly tough. I sent it back and ordered something else. This is actually the only time in my life I've felt compelled to do that. The man to my right asked what it was I sent back. I told him, and he said, "That's what I ordered." He had yet to receive his dinner.

As I waited for my new dinner, the mother at the next table recognized me from an earlier movie I had done and began to pay me effusive compliments on my acting. This went on for a few minutes.

The man to my right was served his dinner. After a moment, he said to me, "I don't know how good an actor you are, but you sure know lousy food."

I Go to Washington

In the midseventies to 1981 I made movies with a big ape, King Kong, a shrinking woman, Lily Tomlin (*The Incredible Shrinking Woman*), and Miss Piggy (*The Great Muppet Caper*).

Ironically, around that same time I became friends with Donald Kendall, who was the CEO of Pepsico as well as the president of the United States Chamber of Commerce, a conservative group that was formed to help business corporations. The two of us flew in his private plane to Washington.

At that time, I was appearing regularly on television, mostly comedically but sometimes as a serious guest, and Don Kendall wanted me to meet members of the incoming Reagan administration and hopefully help get their points of view out there on television. I had a lot of meetings with different groups, and as they explained to me why they wanted to have fewer government programs, I cautioned them on the need for a safety net for the truly needy. I said that the first time someone committed suicide because they had nowhere to turn, it would be a real blow to their policies.

I particularly remember a one-on-one meeting with a very bright young congressman named Newt Gingrich. I remember a phone conversation with Jack Kemp, who later ran for vice president. Congressman Kemp said to me, "I'm aware of what you're doing, and keep it up." I thanked him, even though I had no idea what he meant.

More than one person followed me to the elevator after different meetings, saying no one is talking to us the way you are, and we appreciate the cautionary warnings.

As Don Kendall and I were preparing to leave the capital, a man from one of the meetings came over to me and said, "I'd like to ask you a question." I never wanted to run for office, but I felt I was about to be asked. The man said, "What's it like to work with Miss Piggy?"

The lesson? Watch out for delusions of grandeur.

On the other hand, it's actually been suggested by many people that I run for office. The problem is I refuse to ask people for money, and I don't really travel. I want to help mankind as much as I can from home, or at least within the New York–Connecticut area.

Co-ops

Around the time my wife and I got married, we lived in a two-room apartment that I had lived in alone for about fifteen years. Herb Gardner once came over, looked around, gave me a look, and said, "I know a good lawyer who could get you out of here." My wife gave me a similar look a couple of years later, so we bought a co-op apartment on Fifth Avenue.

I hadn't been trying to save money. I actually *liked* the place. It was on the twenty-second floor. It was quiet. There was a view of the Hudson River from the bedroom, the living room, the kitchen, and the shower. I mean, what'ya *want*!?

For anyone who lives outside the New York area, a co-op is a cooperatively owned building. Each tenant gets a specific number of shares according to the size of their apartment. Every co-op has a board composed of residents who are elected to serve the building's interests. Before you can purchase an apartment in these buildings, you must present yourself before the board so they can determine your worthiness to live in their midst.

We were interviewed by the board. My wife found it

extremely unpleasant, and I found it riveting. When the eighty-something patrician chairman paced back and forth and said, "Your accountant refuses to verify your financial statement," I said, "What? That's the first call I'm going to make after this meeting!" When I called my accountant, he said, "An accountant can't verify his own statement. Who are these people, anyway?!" Great question.

We were accepted into the building, but I have to admit that I was surprised when the board invited me to join them. I had assumed that I wouldn't be welcome in a role like that, because I came to the table with a certain amount of controversy. By that I mean I'm known to have strong opinions, and I'm often around people who don't share them, but I'm a gentleman, so I don't offer my opinion unless asked.

Not surprisingly, after a few meetings another board member pointed at me and said accusingly, "He'd let anyone into the building!" He wasn't far off. My position was that if you could afford it and the police weren't looking for you, why not? On the other hand, some board members considered it a negative that an applicant "gets his clothes off the rack." When I said, "I get my clothes off the rack," they said, "We know." Of course, some of the most disagreeable characters everywhere get their suits *made*.

There are some co-ops in Manhattan, not ours, that will only accept dogs no heavier than fifteen pounds and no taller than twenty-one inches to the shoulder. If there's a question, they'll weigh and measure them, too. The rationale is, "You wouldn't want to get on an elevator and have a Great Dane looking you in the eye, would you?" Not a bad point.

Actually, I don't remember *any* dogs in our building.

The board also used something some called Fidelifacts to investigate applicants. One revealed that a man had been cited in the past for driving the wrong way down a one-way street, which the board chose to interpret as his having a drinking problem, and they were very vocal in not wanting to have anyone with a drinking problem live in the building. I believe it was my friend and fellow board member Gideon Rothschild who then said, "Where are rich people with drinking problems supposed to live?"

Although I was viewed as too open to applicants, I was respected for my dedication to the job, surely evidenced by all my note taking. No one imagined they were notes for a play.

The idea that this needed to be written about had quickly taken hold once I realized that my fellow board members were actually serious about the preposterous concerns raised in our meetings. There were some who felt that the rather elderly doormen should be standing at attention at all times. One board member was certain flowers were being stolen from the arrangement in the lobby and became obsessed with rooting out the supposed thief.

I never witnessed any anti-Semitism in my building, but I know it exists in some exclusive buildings and clubs all over America. A relative in Kansas City was a guest in a private club recently, and someone called out, "What is this, Jew night?" When my Jewish father-in-law was dying with esophageal cancer, I asked his gentile doctor on the phone what had caused the disease. He said, "Eating too much lox." Lox is smoked salmon, which Jewish people particularly seem to enjoy. I took it as an anti-Semitic joke that I'll never forget.

A friend of mine recently bought an apartment on Fifth Avenue and was told he couldn't have a welcome mat outside his door. They allowed him to have his welcome mat inside his apartment.

After we sold our apartment and moved to Connecticut, I began to put on readings of the play I had written about the co-op board. After one of the readings, a former colleague of mine from the board came up to me and said, "Your apartment has tripled in value." I could have said, "So has my house," but I let him have his moment. What does it hurt?

Midnight Run

When people approach me to talk about a movie, it's almost always *Midnight Run*. The real force behind that movie was Martin Brest, who earlier had directed *Beverly Hills Cop* with Eddie Murphy. It was Martin Brest who got Robert DeNiro. It was Martin Brest who got the whole cast, including me, who was the *tough sell*! I did the movie *Isthar* a year before *Midnight Run*. *Isthar* is a movie I like, but it was not a hit, to put it mildly.

Paramount Pictures, the studio that was to finance *Midnight Run*, wanted Cher for my role. You can't make this up!

Martin Brest didn't want Cher. He wanted me, but Paramount wouldn't make it with me, so Martin Brest went to Universal Studios, who said they would.

I had never met Robert DeNiro or Martin Brest when I walked into a hotel room in New York City and spent the next several hours auditioning. Bob and I read the script for Marty. We improvised on the script. I believe there were two such sessions. I may have spent as much as ten hours auditioning with Marty and Bob. Then Marty called me from an airplane. The connection wasn't good, but I gathered he wanted me to come to Los Angeles and audition some more. I asked him what it was he wanted to see that he hadn't seen. The line broke up when he answered, and I chose not to pursue the question.

Instead, I called my agent and told him to tell the studio that I wasn't sure we could agree on a fee, and I named a figure something like four times higher than I'd ever been paid. It worked. Marty Brest called me and said, "If I say you have the part, would you do it for less?" I said, "Absolutely." I give Marty a lot of credit for understanding and respecting that I felt I had auditioned enough.

Marty Brest had no limits on the demands he would make of everyone, which was no problem at all for DeNiro and me, but it was for the cinematographer. In the middle of the movie he decided to quit and of course take his enormous crew with him. I remember walking by Marty as he was talking to the cinematographer in the lobby of a motel in Globe, Arizona. Evidently, Marty felt the cinematographer hadn't given him a good enough reason why he was leaving, and I heard Marty say, "Look, we're making a great movie here, and if you don't want to be part of it we're going to make a great movie anyway." Marty brought in a new cinematographer with a whole new crew.

Neither Bob nor I had ever seen anything like that before, and I, of course, being the talker between the two of us, said to him, "Let's stay out of this, whatever it is, and just concentrate on our responsibilities." We did.

The screenwriter of the movie didn't travel, so sometimes there would be only an outline of a scene, and we'd have to make it up. I remember sitting in a boxcar with Bob who, in the story, was furious with me, and yet the challenge of the scene was that by the end he had to kind of like me. I was handcuffed to something, and I just started to say things to try to amuse DeNiro. It didn't work.

Marty came over and whispered in my ear, "I love you. I think you're great, but this is not working. You've got to come up with something else." I thought for a moment and then asked Bob, "Have you ever had sex with an animal?" That brought his head up, and he stared at me. I then said something like, "I'm asking, because I saw you eyeing one of those chickens on that Indian reservation where we were working." That did it. DeNiro started laughing, and we fulfilled what the scene needed. I credit Marty Brest with continuingly challenging me. At one point Marty told me that DeNiro had come to him and said, "Ya know, Chuck really *is* getting on my nerves." Marty said, "Great!"

I think he's a magnificent director who never really got the credit he deserved for that outstanding picture.

CNBC

In the midnineties, I stopped doing movies so I could be a stay-at-home dad for my son, who was entering first grade.

I began to develop a syndicated show with King World, the people then responsible for *Oprah*, *Wheel of Fortune*, and *Jeopardy* among others, and now *Dr. Phil* as well.

I knew Michael King through my friend John Gabriel. I knew Roger King, the major honcho, because he once joined Dabney Coleman and me when he saw us having dinner together. Roger left his table and sat with us. As the evening was winding down, he offered Dabney and me four thousand dollars a piece if we would fly with him in his private jet to Las Vegas. I think he said four thousand knowing he'd easily go to five. We chose not to go. Looking back, just as with Julie Christie that night who wanted Warren and me to join her and a friend and go somewhere, I'm sorry we didn't. Of course, my biggest mistake in this area was not going on that safari with Johnny Carson.

My idea for the syndicated show at King World was to have a group of humorous people sit around and discuss *whatever*—variations of which have been done in the years since, some successful, some not.

The fellows at King World kept suggesting I have more "elements." I came up with the idea of taking a crew to a stable near Central Park in New York, where I was told there was a horse who could type. We were going to put a typewriter under a horse's hoof. He would then bring his hoof down and, of course, smash the typewriter, and I would be outraged at my producer who had given me the information on the horse's typing ability.

Right around then I got an offer to replace Tom Snyder on CNBC—he was leaving to do a show following David Letterman on CBS. The King brothers graciously let me accept it and didn't ask for any compensation.

Several years later I called Roger King on behalf of a friend of mine, and again he was friendly and gracious. About a month after I called him, I read in the paper that he had died suddenly. I'm sorry I never got to know him better, as I understand he was one of a kind.

I first met Tom Snyder when I was a regular guest on his *Tomorrow Show* in the eighties. One week he was scheduled to go to Egypt to interview Anwar Sadat. The producer, Roger Ailes, suggested I guest host for the week. The Sadat interview fell through, but Tom graciously let me host for the week, anyway.

Tom Snyder was always terrific to me—never competitive, always supportive, and a great audience. That's why I cringe every time I think of something I said to him on the phone when he took a call from me on the air shortly before

I began my show in his time slot. I said I was concerned because there was no studio audience, and if by chance I said something amusing, there would only be silence. I then added, "*You* don't have to worry about that, because you laugh at your own jokes."

There was silence for a second and then we moved on, as though I hadn't said something incredibly rude.

In the last years of his life, Tom and I would talk on the phone, and he sounded the same as he always did—vibrant, high energy, a big personality. Tom had worked for years in radio, and when I started doing commentary on CBS radio I suggested to him that he consider doing a radio show again. He was ill, but I knew he could do it from home. He seemed agreeable, so I made a few calls, but before anything could happen he phoned and said he'd thought more about it and decided he didn't want to do it.

We never discussed his illness, but clearly that had something to do with it, although you'd never know that from listening to him on the phone.

I consider that line about Tom laughing at his own jokes one of the dumbest things I've ever said. The lesson I took away from it is that I who consciously always try to make people feel better am perfectly capable of unknowingly being hurtful. It makes me more vigilant of my own behavior. The problem is we're not aware when we're making mistakes, otherwise we wouldn't make them.

I've unknowingly behaved inappropriately since then, but my rudeness toward Tom still bothers me. May he rest in peace.

When I first came on CNBC at ten o'clock I was supposed to be "the dessert" following Geraldo Rivera, who did nightly panel discussions about the O. J. Simpson case. One day I got a call from an executive at CNBC telling me that the head of the network, Roger Ailes, wanted me to know that Geraldo got a very high rating. He gave me the number. I got a very low rating, and he gave me the number, and the show following mine, which was all about sex, got a very high number. My guest was a person in show business, not the most famous you can imagine. I asked what Roger wanted me to do. He said, "He just wants you to have that information." I said, "Well, if *I* were covering the O. J. Simpson trial or doing shows about sex, I would have a high rating as well." There was a silence, and the fellow on the other end of the phone said, "Roger just wanted you to know." Clearly a polite warning.

Since for me doing shows about sex was out of the question, I began to cover the O. J. Simpson case and soon was getting ratings comparable to Geraldo's. I had now entered the world of lawyers, but it was not my first experience.

That went back about ten years earlier when I was supposed to be doing a movie with a female star, and I was working on the script with the writer for months. At the last moment, the female star withdrew from the picture and the producers decided not to go forward with another actress. If they had called me and given me some explanation, I probably would have let it go at that, but since I had been working on the script with the writer for months for no salary, I decided to sue them, even though there wasn't a signed contract, which in the movie business isn't that unusual. This was the first and only time I brought a suit. I've never been sued.

My lawyers warned me that the attorney for the other side was a real killer. I remember lying in bed in Los Angeles the night before he was to take my deposition and wondering what he could possibly say to me, since I felt I was completely in the right and had worked so long on the script. I imagined him digging out bad reviews from my past and reading them to me, but I'm always prepared for any kind of a confrontation, so even though it was nerve-racking, part of me looked forward to it.

When I entered the room to be deposed, all the lawyers and the producers were sitting there. I looked at their lawyer, and he was a most imposing figure, muscular, big, and very smart-looking. He asked with disdain who *was* I, anyway, to claim that I had worked on the script with the writer! He said, "Are you even a member of the Writers Guild?" He obviously hadn't done his homework. I said, "I am." He sneered at me and asked, "Under what circumstances did you enter the Writers Guild?" I said, "When the Twentieth Century Fox movie studio asked me to write the screenplay of Woody Allen's hit Broadway show *Play It Again, Sam.* He stared at me a moment and said, with some amusement, "Strike my question."

They actually had asked Renée Taylor and Joe Bologna to do the screenplay, but since I had earlier worked successfully with them, they asked the studio if I could join the screenwriting team. When Renée and Joe decided that they would prefer to work on their own script, the studio went forward with me alone.

When I asked one of the executives why they were willing to do that he said, "Well, you were doing all the talking at the meeting, anyway." The movie was to star another actor, because Woody wanted to do two things on the movie, star and write, I assume, but when Woody Allen opened in *Bananas*, a hit movie he had cowritten, starred in, and directed, they decided to go back to Woody to star in the movie version of his play in which he had starred on Broadway. Woody read my script, was very complimentary, but felt it required more of an actor than he was. I didn't agree but thought he had certainly earned the right to write the screenplay of his own hit play, which he did. We went back and forth in the deposition after that, and I believe it all ended with the producer's willingness to pay the costs of my lawyers. I didn't earn any money, but I felt I had made a point. That was my first experience with attorneys.

My experience with them continued later when I was covering the O.J. Simpson case. I had a live debate with Professor Alan Dershowitz, who was on O.J. Simpson's so-called dream team. More than one attorney around CNBC wondered aloud how Charles Grodin, who a year before had been starring in a movie with a Saint Bernard, could possibly debate the renowned Professor Dershowitz from Harvard.

It was an hour and a half debate and the response favored me 85 percent to 15 percent. Of course, it didn't hurt that I was *against* O.J. Simpson. Later, more recently, I ran into Barry Scheck, the head of the Innocence Project with

Peter Neufeld, another member of the dream team. The Innocence Project is a wonderful organization that uses DNA as a way of getting innocent people out of prison. I now support them financially and sometimes write about them for the *New York Daily News* Web site as well as doing commentaries in support of them.

About a year before I became a supporter of the Project, Barry Scheck confronted me at a book party and said that he had watched my show with his teenage son one night a decade earlier and heard me wonder aloud how the defense team could sleep at night. I said, "Someone who does such good work in getting innocent people freed with DNA evidence shouldn't be representing O. J. Simpson." Other words were exchanged, and he turned his back on me and walked away, saying, "You should have more respect for the adversary system." I called after him, "I'm sure you're right." I doubt he knew I was being facetious. Given that he knew how I felt about him, I still can't understand why he'd watch me with his teenage son.

I think the jury system is flawed, because some cases are so incredibly complicated that they are, in my opinion, beyond a layperson's understanding of the law. I believe we should throw it out and have three judges unanimously rule one way or another on cases.

Recently, I was a character witness in a case. The defense attorney described my journalistic background for the past thirteen years, and the prosecutor described me simply as a professional actor. Lawyers want to win, and sometimes it seems to me that the truth is most often secondary—at best.

No wonder I like to watch comedy tapes at night rather than courtroom shows.

At CNBC, there was a regular turnover in executives. Two really stand out. One was a woman who shouted at my producer in a meeting about guests, *"No more old people!"* She was referring to two show business icons who had been my guests. The other was a man who regularly called meetings of the staffs of the shows. I chose never to attend. He seemed to demoralize everyone with his comments and wasn't there very long. He had an odd habit of rocking on his heels as he spoke.

I don't know if these people are out of the business, but I haven't heard either of their names in years.

A startling thing happened when a top executive at NBC called me to say the head of NBC News asked him to tell me that I had stumbled the night before. He meant my rating wasn't at its usual level. I asked him if he had seen the show. He said, "No." That told me that content was irrelevant. The show consisted of the videos I had shot at the Bedford Hills maximum security prison that led to four women being granted clemency. In fairness, he *did* say that whatever I had done could be used in the later part of the show. The show should begin with what today would be called a hot topic. I chose not to follow his advice.

I once had a meeting with this head of NBC News who told me a story about how his friend Don Henley of the Eagles always taped my show if he couldn't see it when it was on. He said Don asked him if he had seen a particular monologue I had done. The man, standing right in front of me, snorted in disdain and said, "Oh, God, no!"—like that was out of the question.

There's an explanation for his rude behavior. It's certainly not exclusive to him. Many people in the news business have a patronizing attitude toward anyone who enters their field from elsewhere. They make false assumptions about lack of qualifications.

The truth is that throughout my life I've followed the news—social and political issues—a lot more than I've followed show business, and I believe the success of my show speaks for itself. Also, I've been asked to broadcast commentary all these years. The people in our country who may have something useful to say obviously are not all working in the news business.

A man whom I've found equally if not more offensive than the network executive is Steven Brill, the founder of Court TV. We've never met, but once we were both at a party at Judge Catherine Cryer's home and I chose not to walk over and speak to him. I would hate to cause discord at someone's party, and discord at least would have erupted had I spoken to Mr. Brill.

He once wrote in a newsletter of some kind that while he found me appealing in the Beethoven movies (a not so subtle dig), he wondered how CNBC could have me sitting in the host's chair. He acknowledged that he had never heard me say anything questionable, "But what if something happens while he's anchoring his show?" Surely, he said, NBC wasn't suggesting that I was in the category of Tom Brokaw or Brian Williams.

I found his observation insulting. I had recently covered the war in Kosovo, where things were *happening* all the time. You talk on a live satellite to the correspondent on the scene, and he tells you what's happening. No one has ever accused me of asking unworthy questions.

This mystifying of what it takes to be a good reporter is a joke. You don't have to be an expert at anything, just know the subject well enough to ask intelligent questions. In my observation, too often the so-called experts aren't experts, and that clearly applies to Mr. Brill.

Ironically, three of my biggest supporters were the three anchors of the network news, Tom Brokaw, Dan Rather, and Peter Jennings, as well as Tim Russert and Jim Lehrer. I say this because they each chose to make it clear to me, not as a result of Mr. Brill's comment but just because they chose to.

If I sound riled up at Steven Brill, it's because I am. That's the effect arrogance has on me.

I debated whether I wanted to put the following story in this book. I felt if Steven Brill's name ever came up in conversation I would share it with friends, and while I undoubtedly won't know most of the people reading this book, I figure if you've come this far, that's friendly enough for me.

Sometime in the nineties, Roger Ailes, who runs the Fox Cable Network and was then running CNBC, put together a whole evening's special with eleven television hosts onstage, most of them notable journalists. Among them was the late Tim Russert.

Roger had me seated center stage with five journalists to

my right and five to my left. We would each host a segment of the evening.

The fella who was second in command to Roger told me that his father called him after the special to say he felt I should have hosted the entire special.

His father was Fred Friendly, Edward R. Murrow's producer and a legend in the news business.

I should have asked Andy to have his dad give Steven Brill a call.

The Rockefeller Drug Laws and the Felony Murder Rule

Here are the two most important things I learned from doing my cable show on CNBC. At this time, and for decades, if not always, politicians who want to appear "tough on crime" have made it legal in New York to set up a sting operation on a young woman on welfare with four small children, no record, and five dollars to her name.

Elaine Bartlett, an African American woman, was approached in Harlem by a police informant, a white man she knew casually who offered her $2,500 to deliver four ounces of cocaine to someone in Albany. The man did this because he wanted a break on his own drug offenses. The police didn't seem to care who was being set up but wanted to build their arrest record.

Despite her boyfriend's warnings, Elaine jumped at the chance. Elaine's son later told me, "We had nothing." On delivering the package, Elaine was immediately arrested. She went to trial and was sentenced to twenty years to life at a maximum security prison.

I was told about the case by Randy Credico, who now runs the William Moses Kunstler Fund for Racial Justice along with Bill Kunstler's widow, Marge.

Randy, who has become a hero of mine, appeared on my CNBC show in the nineties. Another guest was Republican State Senator Dale Volker, a former police officer. When Senator Volker appeared, he took the tough-on-crime position but allowed there could be "some cases worth looking at."

I went to Bedford Hills Correctional Facility for Women, a maximum security prison in Bedford, New York, and did on-camera interviews with Elaine Bartlett and three other young women with no prior records. One was a woman who was also set up by the police. Another was a young woman who was dating a drug dealer, but there was no evidence that she dealt drugs, and the fourth woman was a young mother of two who got hooked on cocaine to lose weight and was taking orders for a drug dealer. None of these women had prior records, and between them they had a number of small children. The state seems to never consider what will happen to the children when their mother is taken away for their entire childhood and longer.

I called Senator Volker and said I'd like to give a lunch in Albany for the Republican leadership and show them the video. One of my producers, John Gabriel, worked with Senator Volker's office to arrange the lunch, and the Republican leadership came, headed by then Republican leader Senator Joe Bruno. I remember one senator said to me, "I've seen your show. If it was up to you, you'd let everyone out of prison." I said, "Nothing could be further from the truth. I believe there are many people on the streets who should be in prison, and I believe there are many people who are let out of prison who never should have been let out."

I showed the video I had shot in the prison and made my case for clemency. Senator Bruno simply said, "I agree with you."

He went to then New York's Governor Pataki. Elaine Bartlett, Arlene Oberg, and Jan Warren were granted clemency that year, and Leah Bundy received it the following year. Elaine had served sixteen years, and the other women had served several years.

Elaine's family was shattered by the experience. Her youngest son took to the streets and was sent to prison. When Elaine's mother died, her oldest son had to leave college, where he had a basketball scholarship, to come home to look after what was left of the family.

Elaine's boyfriend, whom she later married, had warned her and went with her thinking he could somehow protect her. He, too, was arrested, and he served twenty-one years before he was released. He had sold drugs as a teenager, so he got an even harsher sentence. It's hard to express the gratification I feel when I say I was able to get jobs for Elaine and Nathan Brooks when they were released from prison.

Arlene Oberg, one of the sweetest women I ever met, died of a heart attack while still in her thirties.

The Rockefeller Drug Laws under which all these women received mandatory sentences have since been revised but are still unreasonably harsh. They were put into effect to punish drug dealers. Instead, way too often they are used against addicts and desperate people who make a delivery to pay for their addiction.

And it is still legal at this writing to put a police sting on a young woman on welfare with no record who has never even delivered drugs. Shame!

It's hard to top the unintended consequences of the Rockefeller Drug Laws, but we've done it with our felony murder rule, which was intended to cover such examples as when two people go into a bank with guns and one kills someone, both are guilty of murder. I can agree with that.

Brandon Hein was a teenager who didn't kill anyone, but he's serving the same sentence—life imprisonment without the possibility of parole—as the Menendez brothers, who killed their parents; Gary Ridgeway, who killed forty-eight women in Washington state; Sirhan Sirhan, who killed Robert Kennedy; and Charles Manson, although Charles Manson does get to come up for parole. Brandon Hein can't. Ever. So what did Brandon Hein do? He was drunk and got into a fight that involved six boys, one of whom stabbed another, who bled to death. The boy who did the stabbing admitted he did it in an effort to get another boy off his younger brother. The state did not claim that Brandon killed anyone, but under the felony murder rule as applied in this case in California, Brandon was sentenced to life imprisonment without the possibility of parole. How can that be?

Under the felony murder rule, if a jury decides that Brandon and his friends went to a fort in the backyard of a house in Agoura Hills, California, to steal marijuana and not just to smoke it or buy it as the boys claimed, Brandon could be convicted of intended robbery, and that is what the jury decided in spite of the fact that most of the boys knew each other, no one wore disguises, and nothing was taken! Several important factors help explain this gross miscarriage of justice. First, the boy who died was the son of a policeman. Second, the trial took place after the O.J. Simpson acquittal and a hung jury in the Menendez brothers' case. The prosecution badly wanted a conviction. The most important prosecution witness in this case was Mike McLoren, who was with the boy who died and was also stabbed by Jason Holland, who admitted all of this. The witness has been a known drug user and dealer for many years who had lied to the authorities on several occasions before his testimony. Legal scholars have said the sentence for Brandon Hein, who had no prior record, is one of the most outrageous applications of the felony murder rule they have ever seen. If you want to talk about human rights violations, you need look no further than the Centinela State Prison in Imperial, California, where Brandon Hein is in his thirteenth year of incarceration. Brandon began his sentence when he was eighteen. He is now thirty-one. A life sentence with no chance for parole for a teenager who did nothing more than get drunk and get into a fight!

An even more egregious example of the felony murder rule is the story of a boy in Florida who in 2004 lent his car to his roommate, as he had done many times before, and went to sleep. The roommate and others went out and committed a burglary and a murder. *The boy who was home asleep at the time was sentenced to life in prison with no chance of parole!*

The prosecutor said, "No car, no murder." He might have just as well said, "No car dealer, no car, no murder." The boy who lent his car who was asleep in his bed at the time of the crime had no prior record. The prosecution implied that statements the boy gave recalling what he knew when he was drunk the night before implied he was aware his roommate was borrowing his car to commit a crime.

I would feel a lot better about my country if we got rid of the felony murder rule. I don't know of any country in Europe, including England, that hasn't gotten rid of it, as have India and Canada, because it's unjust! A few of our states have gotten rid of it but not California or Florida.

Who's the criminal here? The boy who was asleep in his bed at the time of the crime, or the state that sentenced him to life in prison with no chance of parole? The felony murder rule disgraces America. I can think of many things my country does that disgrace us, and the felony murder rule is right up there.

I hope everyone who reads this tells *everyone* they know about the unintended consequences of the felony murder rule. If a lot of us start talking in our own ways and making phone calls, sending letters, etc., we can make America a better place.

As far as all those politicians who present themselves as tough on crime are concerned, I believe *I'm* tougher on crime than they are. I would make the case as hard as I could to *never* have people who've been arrested several times, sometimes with violence involved, walking the streets. I would *never* have clearly criminally insane people walking our streets but have them in institutions where they at least have a chance to be treated. This is not a job that our corrections officers should be dealing with. They should not have feces thrown at them. My position would always be tougher and fairer. Each case must be looked at individually. One size never fits all. That's why I believe *mandatory sentencing is criminal, and mandatory laws that let people out of prison when common sense says they shouldn't be let out should be eliminated.*

Oh, and by the way, we've never been able to pass an antilynching law in America. The best we've been able to do is have a "nonbinding resolution."

You can't make this up!

How Naïve Can I Be?

I remember telling one of my producers, John Gabriel, the news that my CNBC show had been canceled and replaced by a rerun of *Hardball with Chris Matthews* in June 1998. He was stunned as he stared at me, making sure I wasn't joking, and never took his eyes off me as he reached behind him to feel for the sofa he sank into.

I don't remember any explanation. I told the staff, and everyone was in a state of shock. I immediately took my things and left the building. Later, someone from NBC told me, "You didn't have to leave right away," but, of course, I felt like . . . well . . .

It was shocking, because as was later reported we had been the highest-rated show on CNBC at ten p.m., eleven p.m., and one a.m., often beating CNN. Our program was also the only CNBC talk show to receive a nomination every year for a Cable Ace Award for Best Talk Show.

A couple of weeks later, *New York Newsday*'s columnist Marvin Kitman wrote about the incident, and even more than ten years later, his kind words have stuck with me:

"Charles Grodin, my favorite late night talk show since it debuted January 9, 1995, was abruptly taken from us two weeks ago. After 624 programs the show was sacked by 'Mutual Agreement' or whatever CNBC wants to call what happened the night of June 5th. . . .

The actor/director/author went where no talk show has gone lately. Not only could he make you laugh, but he could make you think. It was an original concept to give an open mike to somebody who could not only speak his mind, but had a mind he could call his own.

His monologues were fascinating because they were so rare. . . . He talked about injustice, welfare, the homeless, the poor. He was using TV to discuss issues. Using it as an educational tool . . . To be fair, as Grodin himself said, CNBC was the only place that allowed him to come on and talk about some of these things, and then 'they only took me off for economic reasons.'

He was one of the things that was good about TV, a genuine original, the closest thing we had to an Oscar Levant."

Marvin thought the reason for my cancellation was an interview I did with Robert F. Kennedy, Jr., the previous November about his book *The Riverkeepers*, which referenced CNBC's parent company, General Electric, polluting the Hudson River. "It was the longest attack on a General Electric–owned network on GE for polluting the Hudson River," Kitman wrote. "Not only had GE dumped PCBs, Kennedy explained, but it was now doing everything in its power not to clean it up. Why? The cost. 'If it was $20,000,' Kennedy said, 'it would have been done 20 years ago. Now they estimate a billion.' But that was nothing like Kennedy's claim that 'Every woman between Oswego and Albany had elevated levels of PCBs in her milk because of GE.' I'm sure that must have thrilled them up there in Fairfield, Conn."

After the cancellation of my show, there was such an immediate, overwhelming outpouring of protests from the viewers that within about a week they called and asked me to come back to host a Friday night show at seven p.m. on MSNBC. Within a year and a half that came to an end as well. By that time I was ready to go, because five years of hosting a show, even if the last year and a half it was once a week, felt like enough.

I should have seen the writing on the wall, because before we were canceled we were moved from ten p.m. to eleven p.m. and replaced by, of all things, reruns of Conan O'Brien, which followed *Rivera Live*, a programming concept that boggled a lot of minds. It was definitely an effort to ease me out. I no longer believe what I said at the time, that it was done for "economic reasons."

One executive at CNBC, Bruno Cohen, whom I liked, told me a sponsor had asked, "Is he going to keep doing those monologues?" Bruno told him, "That's the best part of the broadcast," so I probably offended more people than I can imagine.

Since soon after I left MSNBC I was hired to be a commentator on *60 Minutes II*, I never thought much about what Marvin Kitman had said. But in recent years I've run into two of my former friends from GE/NBC/CNBC at events. One looks at me like I stabbed him in the back. The other looks at me like he was on my side. I've since offered both these people to raise money for one of their charities, but my call wasn't returned, confirming in my mind that what Marvin said in fact was true.

Marvin Kitman summed up his column with the following:

> "Chuck, you did a super job for the last few years. You asked the basic question in your commentaries and interviews: What is going on here? You did it on national TV. It's a credit to GE that it let you do it and a discredit to stop you in mid-sentence, metaphorically. This is a crazy time in history. We need people to sort it out. Some of us may not have liked your approach, but you were doing what TV public affairs should be doing, explaining the insanity of these times to us."

I now agree with Marvin Kitman that the corporation saw Robert F. Kennedy, Jr.'s, appearance as not in their interest, so they tried to stop free speech, but of course free speech is more important than any corporation, and it's not as though Mr. Kennedy's appearance had any impact whatsoever on the strength of GE. Free speech is one of the things that distinguishes America from so many countries, and any corporation that tries to stop it shames itself.

Lousy Treatment of Kids

Right around this time, when my son was ten years old, I became engaged in one of the most dramatic battles I've ever experienced. My boy tried out for and became a player on the fifth-grade travel basketball team.

For those of you who may not know, schools generally have travel teams and intramural teams. You have to try out to be on a travel team. Intramural teams are for any of the kids who want to play. On travel teams the goal is to win. On intramural, while everyone would like to win, there's an understanding that all the kids get equal playing time.

Somehow I ended up on a kind of travel basketball oversight committee. While my experience on the Fifth Avenue co-op board in New York City made quite an impression on me, nothing had prepared me for the travel oversight committee. This hit harder because it was about kids.

It all started innocuously enough. The fifth-grade travel team was coached by a very nice man who was the father of one of the players. Even though we were having a big winning season, as time went on I and a number of others began to see that the best players were seldom on the floor together.

The coach wanted to win but also seemed to have the intra-mural point of view, which meant giving more time to the players who didn't start. One could call this a humanistic point of view.

He was a great guy and all the boys liked him. Still, the oversight committee felt we should follow the established procedure when the fifth-grade team moved to sixth grade. We changed coaches and chose someone who not only had coached before and won but also wanted the best players on the floor as long as possible.

This led to an extremely successful season in which we even won a tournament, but it also led to a different problem. Our sixth-grade coach, also a very nice man, wanted to win so much that the players who didn't start got as little playing time as possible.

A father of one of the boys on the team asked to meet with our committee. He sat at the table and read a letter he had written beseeching us to give his son more playing time. He then got up and left. It was touching to hear, and then the parents of other kids not in the starting lineup who weren't getting much playing time petitioned our committee to address this, and we foolishly put in a rule that all the kids had to play at least eight minutes a game.

Now parents of the kids coming off the bench would sit in the stands with stopwatches to determine if their kids were getting their eight minutes! Often they didn't, and that's when the real anger toward the coach and the over-sight committee began to surface. I spoke to the coach, and the situation got somewhat better but was still not what was promised—those eight minutes for *all* the kids coming off the bench. Anger was building in our town of 18,000. Many people were no longer speaking to each other, or just barely. Mothers were crying.

When the team got to seventh grade, the eight-minute rule was done away with as we investigated and found that none of our travel team competitors had that requirement. But totally unforeseen by anyone, the situation became even worse.

To coach the seventh-grade team, we brought in a man who had done it many times before. He seemed a pleasant fellow, but as I see it, this character appeared to have an agenda. He planned to leave his position to coach another team, the one we ended up playing in our opening game. It was somewhat shocking to see *our* coach coaching our opponent. He had turned the team over to his two assistants, a plan he'd had in place all along. They were both from the area and had played for the high school team years earlier.

Early on, some of our best players were not starting, and not getting substantial playing time, and the team wasn't winning.

I took the two young coaches out to lunch and showed them some newspaper clippings from our previous year when we won a big championship. I didn't want to get in their face. I just showed them the clippings, hoping they'd notice that some of our star players were sitting on the bench. It worked. One fellow said, "You see the same names over and over." I said, "Uh-huh."

One was a very pleasant, laid-back fella, but the other

was more of a tough, somewhat surly man. Very early on the pleasant fella moved on, as his work took him elsewhere, so the rough guy was in charge, and he took over in an aggressive manner we hadn't seen before. Again, these were twelve-year-old boys who loved to play and had been wildly successful the past two years.

Now, this hostile coach, for reasons I'm not qualified to even give an opinion on, was telling one of our best players, as nice a kid as I ever met in my life, to "get off my f— floor." Everyone seemed to be losing their love of the game. It was so bad, I tried to have him removed. I contacted two families who were friends of ours who had boys on the team to support my effort, but they declined. One later wrote me and apologized, belatedly realizing I was right.

Instead, a meeting was called where the coach spoke to the parents. I was so angry I not only didn't speak at the meeting, fearing what I might say, I couldn't even look at him. I do remember him saying, "I coach the way I was coached," and then quoted some horrible stuff a coach had said to him. He did allow how maybe his methods weren't age appropriate, but the hostility and anger from the coach and toward the coach remained in the air.

I really fault myself for not confronting him, since he had the gall to call a meeting. In certain situations in the future I'm going to become more aggressive.

In one game my son was noticeably injured and was limping up and down the court. The coach either didn't notice or didn't care. I walked over to him, said something, and he took my kid out of the game. My boy later was on crutches for quite a while.

The coach continued with his difficult practice exercises, running the boys in what are called suicide drills, where they had to run as hard as they could up and down the gym. In one instance they had to do this five times for every point the other team scored above twelve.

In one game we were ahead by forty points, and all the starters were kept in! Clearly, this guy not only wanted to win, it seemed he wanted to dominate and humiliate the other team.

On other occasions our best players were benched, including one who now plays for a Division One college team. Division One includes the best teams in America. At one point this boy had a couple of games where he wasn't up to his normal level, and the coach chose to read his statistics for those games to the team. Several of the players' attitudes went from "He's okay" to pure hatred.

At another point this strange coach announced that he and the high school coach were going to scout the intramural teams, saying, "I don't know how many of you could play in high school." My son barely played in high school, even though he played for the number-one-rated AAU team in the state that went to the national finals twice. He even won an award.

We were fortunate to get a great guy as eighth-grade coach, but by that time there was so much resentment in the town that some parents just pulled their kids off the team and started another team, weakening our regular team.

The aggressive seventh-grade coach emerged once more in high school coaching girls, and from what I heard, nothing had changed. I sensed that many simply lost their passion for the game and stopped playing.

Abusive coaches who drive kids out of sports aren't unusual. What a disgrace that these apparently unhappy people are put in positions of power—over kids! And they often have no awareness of how inappropriate they are. In fairness, I don't believe our abusive coach realized it, as I've heard that he's a very nice guy when he's not coaching.

Mistakes can be made. The wrong people can be chosen to coach. The real disgrace is that it's allowed to continue once it's recognized, because people didn't stand up and say, "Enough!"

A postscript: In eighth grade the fellows who ran the Parks and Recreation Department of the town who oversaw everything sports-related through eighth grade decided that one of our starting players couldn't play since he was unable to come to the tryouts because of a football injury. I called them and made a case for him, but they said, "If you don't come to the tryouts, you can't play—no matter what the reason."

By then I'd had it! I called a meeting of town officials and the Parks and Recreation people. The eighth-grade coach came and supported my position that the boy should be allowed to try out when his injury had healed. The high school coach came and also agreed with me, as of course did the boy's father.

The Parks and Rec people said about me, "He wants this

boy to have another chance to try out because he's one of the stars, but he wouldn't be for it if he was just another kid who was injured, and a rule is a rule." I said, "I'd be for giving *any* kid a chance to try out if he was injured when the tryouts were held." It was a standoff. The town officials said they'd let us know of their decision in a day or two.

I then got in my car and headed to New York where I was working for *60 Minutes II*. Driving in, I thought to myself I could have made a better case, so from my car I called my assistant and dictated an e-mail I wanted her to send to the town officials. In it I told the whole story of the past three years and the drama and trauma, and basically said, "Enough is enough!" They decided to let the boy try out. He made the team and had a great season! I guess all's well that ends well, but not really.

Highly Unusual
Experiences
That Make Me Not Miss
Show Business

I once worked with a star actor who replaced another star in a play I was featured in. After the stage manager ran through a rehearsal of a scene with the two of us, the actor asked me what I thought. I said I didn't think it was appropriate to comment on what a fellow actor was doing.

He said, "I'm *asking* you!" I replied, "I think you're coming off too angry." He said I'll give you a buck for every laugh (and then he said the star's name he was replacing). "I'll give you a buck for every laugh I don't get that he got!" Well, on his first night in the scene with me, he didn't get one laugh, and then he was angry at *me* for the rest of the run, and I didn't even ask him for some bucks!

Another star who followed that actor in the play once told me he wanted to see me in his dressing room after the performance. He was livid as he circled me—I was standing in the center of the room. I had no idea what was going on and told him so. He said, "You're trying to make me look *gay!* I told him I honestly had no idea what he was talking about. I think he saw I meant it, and amazingly, he immediately dropped his anger and walked away.

I later learned that irrational outbursts were not unusual for him.

One of the strangest experiences I've had came early on in the first play I wrote. It was done in Nyack, New York, in 1971, and all the actors were asked to wear their own clothes, as if they were going to a social gathering.

One actress showed up at dress rehearsal with a dress that looked as if it were made of a hundred shiny mirrors shooting light in every direction.

I drove most of the cast from New York City to the theater in Nyack and back. On the way home after the dress rehearsal I said to the actress, who was sitting in the backseat, "Would you wear a dress that's, uh, a little more conservative?" She said, "That's the only dress I have." I said, "That's your only dress?!" She said, "That fits. Yes." I said, "Buy a dress, and I'll pay for it." She said, "There won't be time for alterations."

I suddenly felt I was in the middle of some neurotic game, so I stopped talking about it. When I dropped her off at her building she said, "So what do you want me to do about the dress?" I said, "I've said everything I can say."

At the next rehearsal, she showed up with exactly the kind of dress that was needed.

Ironically, this actress went on to become quite famous, but recently when I mentioned her name to another actress, she just about turned white. I chose not to pursue the conversation, but I'm sure I'm not the only one, for reasons best known to the actress with the mirrored dress, with whom she chose to play strange games.

I recently looked up my name in a memoir she wrote, and her description of the play was that it was written by the actor Charles Grodin, but the money wasn't there to take it to New York, which I took as a subtle dig. I'd never had a thought about New York at that time. Again, it was my first play. Ironically, twenty-one years later it *did* open in New York and was very successful, with a good review from the *New York Times*, which she chose not to mention in her memoir. In fairness to her, she may not even have known that.

One leading lady was going through a difficult time with her boyfriend during filming a movie and barely spoke to me or anyone else for months. Not fun. I was the writer and male lead of the movie, and one day the leading lady, whom I had chosen for the role, said to me, "Why do you have all the lines in this scene?" They were expository lines that were needed to explain the complicated plot. I said, "Would you like them?" She said yes, so I gave her all the expository lines, and when she saw herself on the screen looking at the dailies (the previous day's shooting), she looked at me like I had pulled a fast one on her. In fact, I was just trying to get through the day with her.

I was on location in another country with a most unusual director on a movie. He always seemed angry and agitated. One day I asked him what was bothering him. He said that I and the other two leading actors had motor homes, and he had something significantly smaller. I said, "You can use my motor home anytime you want." I didn't sleep in the motor home, so I had no problem sharing it, particularly if it would calm him down.

Sometimes when I would be in my motor home with someone, he would burst in, not speak to anyone, open the refrigerator, guzzle down a large bottle of juice, then storm out, still without saying a word.

We once had a scene where there was a violent shoot-out. There were explosives rigged all over the bedroom as Farrah Fawcett and I crawled across the floor—Farrah, bare-legged. I said to the director, "This feels a little too violent." He said with disdain, "It's in the nature of the shot." Farrah ended up bleeding from about twenty places on her legs.

At the party to celebrate the completion of filming, the director brought a woman who was dressed as though she might be a prostitute. He danced wildly with her while holding a bottle of scotch, like in a bad movie. Then he joined the producers and their wives, the other actors, and me at a table with his date, still not speaking. Not exactly the boy next door, not even close.

For reasons known only to him, he would say to his assistant, referring to me, "Ask our star to come to the set." In a fight scene an actor accidentally broke my nose. It didn't really hurt, so I said, "Let's keep shooting." He said, "You're showing me something." I have no idea what I showed him before that, but he stopped referring to me patronizingly as "our star."

Then there was the producing couple who said about a movie I'd written, "We're going to do your movie." Two weeks later I heard they weren't going to do my movie. I phoned and said to the guy, "I thought you were going to do my movie." He said, "When we say, 'We're going to do your movie,' that doesn't mean we're going to do your *movie.*"

I once read an entire movie script I had written to a producer at his home. I played about thirty roles, men and women. He fell asleep about three-quarters of the way through, woke up at the end, and proclaimed, "I'm going to make this movie!" Later, when he became head of a studio, he *did* make the movie. My agent, who was negotiating the deal on my behalf, suddenly left the agency business and joined the studio that he'd been negotiating with. He then proceeded on more than one occasion to be openly hostile to the movie. When it was finished, I heard that he told the studio head, my former producer, that the movie was a catastrophe. Happily, when the studio head saw it he loved it.

Once I was sitting at a screening of this same movie with the director and my former agent, now studio executive. In one scene there was an audio cut, something common in movies, where a character on-screen is describing someone. The audio continued over a shot of the man he was describing, who was sitting in a car on a stakeout.

My former agent called out angrily from the back of the screening room, "The audio is still on from the previous screen!" I responded, in a little angrier tone than he had used, "It's *supposed* to be!"

I don't know if that guy is still in the business, but I haven't heard his name in decades.

I once worked with a movie director who told me in a meeting before we began filming that he tends to scream at people. When I stared at him, he said, "I wouldn't scream at *you*." I suggested it wouldn't be in his interest to scream at anyone. When we began filming, he began screaming, and he was soon fired. It didn't help his cause that when he filmed a scene in which it was supposed to be raining, it was raining on only one side of the street. Clearly, screaming wasn't his only problem. I heard he had gotten some strange injections in Europe.

When I was making the movie *Catch-22* in Mexico in the late sixties, some of the people working on it got into a scuffle with some of the local Mexican guys. I was told that the Mexican police who were assigned to our movie asked our producers if they should speak to the local people or kill them. The producers opted for speaking. Years later, I was making another movie in Mexico. I asked a young Mexican woman assigned to the movie as a translator out for dinner. She told me she had just broken up with her boyfriend, having learned he was married, but she felt obligated to tell me he was very jealous.

I said, "You learned he was married?! What right does he have to be possessive of you?"

She again said he was very jealous, and then added he was a policeman. I immediately remembered what I was told about the police years earlier, but I had too much pride to act as though I was concerned. Somehow, though, I managed to turn our proposed dinner date into a lunch with her—and her sister.

When I began the movie I was shown an incredibly luxurious penthouse suite with a balcony that seemed to overlook all of Acapulco. You entered through a stairwell on the road. I said, "I can't stay here." Everyone looked at me, baffled. I said, "There are bandits in the mountains right behind the stairwell. They can easily come down out of the mountains and do whatever." They reassured me sufficiently that I chose to stay there. During the movie, bandits came down out of the mountains, stole the car that was assigned to Farrah Fawcett, and killed her driver.

Why I'm Getting
Increasingly Skeptical

As I'm sure is clear by now, I was able to move ahead in show business by believing my version of what was happening and not someone else's just because that someone happened to be in authority.

I've seen it everywhere. From the President of the United States to the man who unsuccessfully tried to fix our refrigerator, it's not unusual for people to not know what they're doing.

This, of course, is true in personal relationships as well. If a significant number of people see you a certain way, there's probably truth in the perception, but if it's *one* person who has an opinion of you that no one else seems to share, that person needs to look more at themselves. I know of so many relationships that have gone bad because people were unable to do that. That should be a goal for all of us. It's easy to point fingers. It's obviously much more difficult to take responsibility. "The truth, the whole truth, nothing but the truth" may be the biggest challenge for all of us.

When I was a boy, I was told it was a good idea to put my savings into a savings account where my money would earn interest and someday turn into significantly more money than I started with, so I gave the same advice to my son when he was fifteen. He put the money he had accumulated from gifts from various relatives over the years into a savings account at our local bank, and we let it sit. When we went to withdraw the money from his savings account, we were looking forward to seeing how much interest he'd earned. We were surprised to see his account held *less* money than he had put in because the bank had charged him $15 a month for an inactive account, more than the interest the bank paid, which was less than 1 percent.

So my son paid the bank for taking his money and investing it for their own gain. They made money off my son and charged him for it.

That ought to be illegal.

For as long as I can remember, I've been more skeptical of things than most people, but in the last thirteen years or so, working for NBC and CBS News, my skepticism has quadrupled—at least—beginning with stories about myself that I've read in the papers or seen on the news that have no truth to them at all.

Reports had me attending Robert Blake's wife's funeral in Los Angeles in 2001. I haven't been to Los Angeles since the early nineties. Mrs. Blake was known to have put nude photos of herself on the Internet to attract male clients—not a group I'd want to be associated with.

Once, at a party, I was told by a journalist that I had written a very angry letter to someone complaining that I wasn't recognized sufficiently at an event. I had no idea what he was talking about. I asked him to give me a source. He looked into it and then reported to me it wasn't an angry letter, it was "a series of irate phone calls." I don't think anyone in the history of show business, including Joan Crawford or Bette Davis, has made "a series of irate phone calls" about not being recognized somewhere. The fact is, I prefer to not even go out. Yet that story was making the rounds. In fact, I'm widely known for my lack of irateness. Irate is just not one of my things. I'm not saying I don't *have* things. I'm just saying, irate is not one of my things.

I was recently sent a biography of me to check before an event I was hosting. It said my mother's last name was Moretsky. That's not true. It said her father's name was Emanuel Moretsky. That's not true. It said I made my film debut in an uncredited role in Disney's 1954 film *20,000 Leagues Under the Sea.* I not only was uncredited, I wasn't in it. If the picture was released in 1954, it was probably made in 1953, when I was still in high school and then started college. It said I hosted *Saturday Night Live,* and before the show the writers and I decided to play it as if I had missed dress rehearsal and was clumsily ad-libbing my way through the sketches. It said the comic scenario was taken a bit too literally by the audience, and I was never asked to host again. That *Saturday Night Live* is one of the shows they put out on the *Best of Saturday Night Live* DVDs, and, of course, I have been asked to host the show again. It said that among other books I wrote is one titled *Spilled Milk and Other Clichés.* I've never even heard of the book.

Not that long ago I read an article in the *New York Daily*

News about the second President Bush that stated he had wanted to marry another woman before he met his wife, Laura. The article said the woman didn't want to marry him because she had wanted to marry Charles Grodin, and she hadn't gotten over that that didn't happen. This was a woman I had gone out with, but I had no idea she wanted to marry me, and I seriously doubt that she hadn't gotten over me when she met the future president, because the last time I saw her was at a party at her apartment and she was sitting in a corner kissing another guy.

What Did You Say?

Maybe it's because the last book I worked on was about learning from our mistakes that lately I'm thinking more about mistakes I and others have made. First, the others.

I remember once meeting the movie director Robert Altman. The meeting was set up because he liked improvisation in his movies, and I had a reputation for being good at it. Five minutes into the meeting he said to me, "I know I should like you, but I don't." I know that was because he didn't sense even the slightest bit of deference from me. Again, no one has either felt the slightest bit of superiority from me, either.

I told Herb Gardner about my meeting with Robert Altman. He said, "That's strange, because when I was laid up with my back, he stood at the foot of my bed and talked for about an hour about backs." I said, "Well, he's comfortable in the position of authority." Herb, who was seldom at a loss for words, simply said, "Oh."

I believe Robert Altman was an extremely gifted director, and I've never heard anyone say one bad thing about him. Quite the contrary. But I found there was that need to feel slightly superior, which in my mind is a flaw many people have. Not a way to win friends and influence people, at least not with me.

A television executive in New York told me he'd call me back in six minutes. It's been a couple of years now, and I'm still waiting. However, I try not to take these things personally. I know if they're happening to me, I'm sure I'm not alone.

I've learned over the years something that should be obvious to all of us, but I don't think it is. It's much easier to *feel* offense than to know we're offending, because the hardest person to see is ourselves.

I was talking to a producer in Los Angeles on the phone about a play of mine he chose not to do. It was all very pleasant, actually. I'd never met the man, so I was surprised when he said at the end of the conversation, "I'll call you next week. I don't want a week to go by without hearing your voice."

Well, a lot of weeks went by without him hearing my voice. I called him about three months later about another project, and when he got on the phone he quite seriously said, "Boy, you don't give up, do you?"

I try to find things amusing whenever possible, and in a short time I found that funny. That's not to say I don't also find it offensive. I'm sure he had no idea he was rude.

In a later conversation, when I called him on behalf of a friend, I told him I was going to put the above story in a book, but I wouldn't use his name. He urged me to use it, but I feel it will make him look foolish, which I don't want to do, especially since more than one person has told me he's a very nice guy. Sometimes we obviously don't know what's best for us.

In my most recent conversation with him on the phone (I still have never met him), he interrupted me and rudely said, "Let's cut to the chase." I was calling him about a script I'd put together from transcripts about Brandon Hein and the consequences of the felony murder rule. I wanted him to have readings of it once a week when they didn't have a play on, as his theater is close to where the crime took place. I'd already had readings of it in New York. He wrote to me speaking glowingly of the play, but for reasons I couldn't follow chose not to do it. His salutation was, "Love ya!"

There's always been a feeling that there's a lot more show business phoniness in Los Angeles than in New York. I wouldn't be a good judge of that, because I've never been out or around much on either coast, but in my limited experience I'd say it's true.

That doesn't mean there's not appalling behavior on both coasts. I had occasion recently to call the head of a theatrical agency in New York about a friend. Before I could even get to the reason for the call, he said to me, "You know, when you were a commentator for *60 Minutes II*, they auditioned two of my clients to replace you."

That was highly unlikely, since before I resigned from the broadcast I had just been given a very substantial raise, but even if it were true, why say it? In a later conversation he went on to show that his insensitivity during the first call wasn't a fluke. I'm sure he has no idea how offensive he is. There are many people who feel the need to establish themselves as superior because, whether they're aware of it or not, they feel inferior.

Perhaps the most offensive thing I've ever had said to me came from an executive at MGM who released my movie *Movers & Shakers*. Richard Graff asked me on the phone, "Do you have a match?" I said, "A match?" He said, "Yeah, burn the print, nobody wants to see your movie." Later I learned the studio made money on the movie because of its low cost and because enough people wanted to see it that almost twenty-five years later it's still being shown on cable.

I did have the satisfaction of calling Alan Ladd, Jr., the head of the studio at the time, and telling him of my conversation with Mr. Graff, whom I'm sure got an earful from his boss.

Some people cross a line so egregiously that retribution is a must.

Proceed with Caution

On several occasions *I've* offended people, and I have no idea I've done it. My first memory of this was when Laurence Olivier came backstage to meet me after seeing a play I was in. I don't remember if he had his title then. He was with a woman, and I talked with him about the grind of doing eight performances a week. He said, "It's not for us to enjoy, it's for the audience."

Later, I heard the woman was appalled at how I spoke to Sir or not Sir Laurence. I have no idea what she was referring to. Laurence Olivier didn't seem appalled at all. I think it probably offended her because I treated him as an equal, which as I've said is how I've always treated everyone. This makes me popular with doormen, for example, and sometimes less popular with people who expect you to look up to them. I don't look up or down at anyone, just straight ahead, and my feelings about everyone have nothing to do with their status, only their character.

Several decades ago I was sitting with a group of people that included two world-famous composers. One of them was a close friend of mine. The other was famous for Broadway musicals. My friend said to the other composer, "I'm thinking of writing a Broadway musical. Could we have lunch sometime? I'd like to pick your brain." The Broadway icon acted as though he didn't hear my friend, but clearly he had.

When the Broadway composer didn't respond, I said, "He just asked if you'd have lunch with him." Again there was no response, but later I heard that over the years whenever my name came up in this composer's presence he makes his feelings about me clear, and they're not good. Obviously, I had offended him, but I still think I was right to speak up.

About five years ago, a friend of mine who was a major league baseball pitcher called me from his car on the way to a ball game. He said the name of a future Hall of Fame pitcher who was sitting with him. Probably because I was focusing on our conversation, I rudely neglected to say something flattering to the other pitcher. A few years later I met the Hall of Famer at a gathering, and I apologized. He told me to forget it, but it was clear he hadn't.

Some recent events come to mind. Once I was hosting a local musical show and introduced an amateur singing group, which by the way was excellent, by saying in a misguided effort to be amusing, "Because you don't have to audition for this group should in no way reflect on its quality." The audience laughed, but the group was extremely offended. I feel very bad about that. I'm no longer asked to host that event.

I was once hosting an event at the Maritime Aquarium in my area. I began by apologizing in advance if I offended anyone, because that was not my intention.

I chose not to do any fish jokes, because I couldn't think of any and had no great desire to try. I then introduced the new head of the aquarium as "probably the most offensive of us all." I don't think that offended the lady, because she knew we had just met. There really was no opportunity for either of us to unknowingly offend.

They were giving awards to banks and families in the area who had given money and done good deeds. One woman donor gave a very serious speech that ran three times longer than anyone else's. As she walked away, I returned to the podium and said, "*Very* funny." That was it! The audience laughed, but it was inappropriate. I'm not exactly banned from appearing at the aquarium, but let's just say I'm not their first choice to host—or second or third.

Another time I spoke at a book party for Ellen Burstyn at the Carnegie Foundation. I wasn't aware I'd said anything offensive until my publisher called the foundation to arrange for a book party for the last book I worked on. They were told in effect that the foundation was booked every night for years to come. This *really* bothers me when I think I might have unknowingly offended Ellen, for whom I have nothing but fondness. I know I said I had to leave to see the New York Giants play football on television. On second thought, that really *is* offensive. The lesson? Think at least three times about doing or saying something that can be taken different ways. Kind comedy is the toughest. Ask Don Rickles.

More recently, a friend asked me if I would moderate a discussion about the European Union at the New York Public Library. I said I really didn't know anything about the

European Union. My friend said this was all scripted, and different actors would play the roles of intellectuals from different European countries using the intellectuals' own words on the European Union.

I got the script and found it fairly obtuse. I asked if I could meet the people at the library to gain a better understanding of the event. When I did, I asked them what percentage of their audience they felt would understand all of this. One man said about 8 percent. There was laughter and jokes all around, and I agreed to do it.

On the night of the event one of the people from the library approached me and the other members of the company to say there would be a European supermodel (whatever that means) arriving at some point in the evening, and when she arrived we were to stop our presentation so she could say a few words.

When I realized he wasn't joking, I said incredulously, "You actually want us to stop our performance so a European supermodel can say a few words?" The man stared at me a moment, went away to consult with one of his colleagues, then came back and said that on second thought we shouldn't stop our performance if the supermodel were to arrive in the middle of the presentation.

Happily, she arrived before the performance and gave a little speech.

I felt the show went extremely well. The actors representing the various European intellectuals were masters at their dialects, and the audience really seemed to enjoy the evening.

Afterward I phoned the fella at the library to see how he felt about it. Generally, people call me after an event, but he didn't, so I called. When the call wasn't returned, I phoned again. From his assistant's attitude it was clear there would be no return call, and there never was. Just one of the many situations where I unintentionally offended, even though I have no idea how.

I'll try to be more careful.

Socializing

In recent years I don't much like to go out in the evenings, even locally, but sometimes I feel that I have to show up at friends' dinner parties or they'll think I'm mad at them or something. I can have a good time when I go out, but for me, as for a lot of people, the looser the better. I honestly think this attitude of "leave me alone" started unconsciously with my resentment at "single file, no talking" in grammar school.

I particularly don't like sit-down dinners or place cards or all those rules, which, of course, offends the people who do like them. Some hostesses at sit-downs want you to sit there for a pretty long stretch after all the courses. It seems to me men have a tougher time doing that than women. As I walk around, I sometimes peek into the dining room and see the men who are too afraid to get up sitting there in what to me looks like pain.

The only kinds of dinner party rules I like are come when you want, or don't. That's okay, too. Walk around when you want, leave when you want. That's my "do unto others." Y'know the classic novel *Great Expectations*? I have *no* expectations. It's more relaxing. I'm not saying I'm right about this, but I bet there are millions of people who feel as I do. The *really* tough sit-down place-card deal is when at some point the hostess or host asks everyone to respond to a question. A recent one was "How did you meet your spouse?" No big deal, right? It was for me. I can't really tell you why. I just know that as the people around the table dutifully told their spouse meeting stories I was silent, then tense, then I started making jokes.

Stuff like "I don't for a minute believe that's how you met him."

Graciously, I hope, I managed to leave the table before my turn came. I have a pretty good spouse meeting story, too, which I'm going to tell you. I just didn't feel like sharing it with a group of people, some of whom I barely knew. I can write about it, but that feels different.

Generally, I choose to share that only with close friends who probably already know how I met my spouse.

I think what I just said is fairly defensible, but my behavior at one dinner party wasn't.

Even though I have a tendency, like most of us, to be on *my* side, in this one even *I* can see I was out of line. The host asked everyone their thoughts on the election. It wasn't take your turn as we go around the table and it wasn't obligatory, although a few times the host looked at me and said, "Chuck?"

I asked the host if I could use his treadmill, then got up and left the room. I actually thought about using the treadmill but chose to just sit in the living room, where the hostess soon joined me. She didn't want to discuss the election, either.

I know this, though. As bad as I am with all of the above, if anyone ever starts a game of charades, the sound of tires screeching into the night means Charles has left the building.

Regrets

The book of mine that is most often referred to was my first. *It Would Be So Nice If You Weren't Here: My Journey Through Show Business* was about what to do if they keep telling you to get lost. Well, if not "Get lost," certainly almost *never* "Come here."

In hindsight I should have said I had a consistent number of what would be called minor successes along the way. In other words, to eventually succeed, more than one person has to notice you can be good, and it can't be family members. In 1953, the head of the department of drama at the University of Miami, Lee Strasberg six years later, and, in between, a lot of people of so-called lesser stature took note of me.

If about 5 percent or less of us entering show business make a living, think hard about whether you can be in that 5 percent. If you think so, then try. But don't grow old trying! People who know more about this than I do estimate that 1 or 2 percent out of millions achieve significant success.

That's a message I wish I'd made clearer in my first book, because I'm afraid I might have encouraged people to stick with it who possibly would have been better served not doing that after a period of time. Again, you don't want to grow old trying.

If it hadn't been for Mike Nichols, would Dustin Hoffman have had the career he's had? If it hadn't been for Mel Brooks, would Gene Wilder have had the career he's had? If it hadn't been for Elaine May, would I have had the career I've had? As I've already said, you can be really good at what you do and not make a living in show business.

Have more than one field if you can. Being in show business really allows that because so few people work but so many are really good. It can be a heartbreaking profession.

Another regret I have, I wish I had realized earlier that if a friend wants to borrow money, if you can afford to, give it rather than loan it. Unless the friend absolutely insists it has to be a loan, which only one friend of mine did, make it a gift.

It is not that unusual for friendships to end because the person who has borrowed the money and can't repay it disappears from your life out of embarrassment. This happened to me with a woman friend who wanted to borrow some money to videotape her father in his later years. I lent it to her and never heard from her again.

I was at a dinner party at a restaurant where the host and everyone went someplace afterward to hear one of the guests speak about the state of the world. I'm not really interested in going out to hear *anyone* speak on the state of the world, *especially* after being out for a couple of hours at dinner, and I *know* I offended the speaker by not joining the group to hear him. Most likely he wouldn't have believed the truth, so I should have said on arriving that I had to leave after dinner. Maybe I could have said I was going to perform a tonsillectomy or have one performed on me—*something*.

Many years ago I had two women friends. We were as

close as anyone could be. Eleni Kiamos, the friend who did so much for me in the early part of my career, died of colon cancer in her fifties. I first saw Eleni excel as an actress on a live one-hour television show, while I was still at the Pittsburgh Playhouse. Eleni believed in putting her faith in the Lord. She contracted colon cancer. When she told me her symptoms, I persuaded her to see a doctor, but it was too late.

I met Luanna Anders a decade later. Luanna once came to visit me when I was making a movie in Mexico. We were in the swimming pool one night, and she said she was taking a writing class and had a new boyfriend. Since Luanna and I were never romantic, I asked what she was doing in Mexico with me. She said simply, "You asked me to come, Chuck." Luanna put our long-term friendship ahead of her writing class and new boyfriend.

She developed breast cancer, and just as Eleni had, she chose not to see a doctor but to put her faith in her religion. By the time she saw a doctor it was too late.

There's no solace for me in that story except to say that the man who was Luanna's new boyfriend in 1978 remains one of my closest friends to this day. My wife and I are guardians to his and his wife's children.

I miss Eleni and Luanna so much that even though they've been gone for decades I remember their phone numbers without needing to look them up. As I've said, I deeply regret I wasn't sufficiently aware of Herb Gardner's smoking. It's less odd that I knew nothing of my female friends' health issues, but I *so* wish I had.

Peter Falk

One of my favorite people is Peter Falk, who as well as being unique is wise. Unfortunately, at this writing, he's suffering from Alzheimer's.

When I turned fifty, I started to get in touch with my mortality in a really uncomfortable way. I asked Peter his feelings on the subject, and I'll never forget his answer: "I figure if so many people have done it [died], I can do it." It actually helped—a lot.

I once asked him to star in a movie I wrote. He loved the writing but said, "Nothing happens in this movie." It was made, but Peter was right. It really wasn't what we expect from a movie.

One day I took him to spend some time at Walter Matthau's house. They had met but didn't really know each other. As we left, I asked Peter what he thought of Walter. He said, "I never know what to say to Walter. I just don't know what would interest him."

Peter's greatest charm is his ability to be interested in just about anything, a trait in which I'm sorely lacking. At a New Year's Eve dinner I sat a close friend next to him. Afterward,

I asked her what she thought of him. She said, "He's more interested in what I have to say than I am."

As big a treat as he was on *Columbo*, he was an even bigger treat in person.

Henry

O f course, it's an inevitability of life that as we get older we lose loved ones. In my experience it's most unusual that we would also gain new loved ones, but that's what happened to me ten years ago when I met Henry Schleiff, who now runs the Hallmark Channel.

It certainly wasn't love at first sight. He was working for a television syndicator and wanted to meet me to discuss co-hosting a morning talk show with the beloved Dana Reeve, Chris's wife. We met in my agent Jimmy Griffin's office. Henry sat on a sofa, Jimmy sat behind his desk, and one of my producers, Clay Dettmer, sat on a chair to my left.

Henry first said the show would air at nine a.m., which was when my close friend Regis Philbin was on with Kathie Lee. Even though I knew it was out of the question, because I would never compete with a friend, not to mention lose to Regis, I didn't interrupt, as Henry had clearly prepared for this meeting, which he proved by pulling an envelope from his jacket pocket and began to read to me scribbled notes he had written on it.

Surprisingly, they weren't notes about his ideas for the

show, but criticism of me as host of my nighttime cable show. I could see Jimmy and Clay eyeing me warily, waiting to see if I'd get up and leave—or worse—but I was so taken with Henry's nerve that I didn't interrupt him.

He said he felt my monologues sometimes ran on too long. I didn't disagree, so I didn't say anything. He wondered what I was looking at when I sometimes looked to my right of camera, where someone was standing with a note on a card reminding me of my next subject. That was something I soon abandoned, so even though I again didn't disagree, I still didn't say anything, because I was marveling that a stranger was giving me all these notes without being asked.

I chose not to do the morning show, but it was an odd beginning to a relationship that was to become so important.

I next ran into Henry at an event for our mutual friend Regis. He approached me with his wife, Peggy, who also became a dear friend. He knew that I was very close to a legendary broadcaster, and he wanted me to tell my friend that he was welcome to do anything, anytime, for Court TV, which Henry was then running. I told him my friend had retired and wasn't interested in coming back to TV. Peggy then said to Henry, "Why don't you invite Chuck to do whatever he wants on Court TV?" Henry paused for a moment and then said, "Sure." That's all.

Sometime later I asked to meet with him. His head of daytime programming, Marlene Dann, who had been my wonderful producer at CNBC, was there with another woman. I told Henry about the interviews I conducted with women who were in prison under the Rockefeller Drug Laws.

The time was getting close to a decision on clemency, so I said I felt it might be useful for me to interview the women's children on Court TV and send those interviews to Albany to perhaps help the cause. When I finished talking, Henry leapt to his feet and basically repeated everything I had just said, except he did it pacing around with great excitement and waving his arms. I found it odd and strangely charming. When I left, I had a feeling this program was going to happen, but I heard nothing for a week or so. I called Marlene Dann to ask what was up. She said, "When you left, Henry turned to me and said, 'He's going to cost a lot of money.'"

I called Henry and asked him if money was an issue. He said it was. I said, "How about I do it for nothing?" That was always my intention anyway. He quickly replied, "It's a deal." I interviewed two kids, sent the video to Albany, and it definitely helped in getting clemency for their mothers.

I began to run into Henry at various events and realized that he was the single funniest person I'd ever met. That was a big deal for me. We began to chat on the phone, and he would *consistently* say things that I would write down and would ask his permission to use in a play I was writing.

Here's an example: it's absolutely true, and no name is changed. A friend of ours had a colonoscopy. Henry went into the recovery room and told our groggy friend, "Everything's fine. There's one slight complication. Doctor Schmeerin can't find his watch."

Once Henry called me after he had hernia surgery and said, "I'm not allowed to laugh. That's why I called you." Most of his jokes are on himself and his bad golf game. He told me recently that people call his club wanting to know when he's playing so they can have a winning day.

Along with his unending humor, he has also stepped over the line twice with me in recent years. I called him on it both times, and he more than made up for it in the following weeks. In my experience, that's not necessarily the norm.

He had Ethel Kennedy call me to host an event at her house. She said, "I hear you're not only highly respected, but beloved." I said, "Can I ask you a question?" She said, "Sure." I asked, "Who is this *really*?"

For me, and I'm sure for most everyone to have someone in your life who is not only a tremendous human being, a wonderful father, and also consistently hilarious is like a dream.

Oh, yeah. Henry read an earlier draft of this book and told my editor, "This can't be the final draft, because I'm not in it."

Now, he deservedly is.

Jack Paar
and Regis Philbin

I remember first appearing on Regis's show in Los Angeles in the seventies. The movie *Heaven Can Wait* had come out. Regis said there was talk of my getting an Academy Award nomination and asked if I was going to do anything to promote that idea. I said, "Other than the blimp, no."

The movie received eleven nominations. I wasn't nominated. Maybe the blimp wasn't a bad idea. I've never really been able to get behind the whole award thing, although I've never turned one down. I mean, you could have an elderly man competing against a teenager for Best Actor. Maybe if everyone played the same part I could buy it, but, of course, there are drawbacks to that concept.

Through the years I continued to appear with Regis and a number of different cohosts. Kathie Lee and I had and have a warm relationship, as I do with Kelly. Somewhere along the way, I became friends with Regis and Joy, who by the way *is* a joy. The degree of interest she has in what I say is deep and sincere, and in that way she reminds me of Peter Falk. She is Regis's protector in every way you can imagine. "Don't have that dessert," and just love—lots of love.

Regis is special. What you see is what you get, which is great. Recently, I asked him as a joke to be part of my senior advisory board, and he asked, "Why does it have to be called senior?"

Regis, Joy, my wife, Elissa, and I have dinner together every couple of months and Regis and I have lunch together around the same number of times. These are memorable occasions for me. I've been out in public with household names, but I've never seen anything like it is with Regis. It seems as though everyone knows him, and it sure feels like everyone loves him. He stops at a number of tables before he gets to me at a back booth. Everyone greets him, and he greets everyone. There are continuous warm exchanges, and he never hurries to get away.

Then, when he's seated with me, he's recognized by more people. He always points to me and says, "You know who this guy is sitting here? Did you see *Midnight Run* with Robert De Niro? This is Charles Grodin, the guy with De Niro." Often the people start to fuss over me. The whole thing is a trip. Not only that, Regis is either funny or interesting and mostly both, and if there's a problem, usually with my talking about social issues, here's what happens. Recently, I asked him to join me in a benefit for our veterans returning from Iraq and Afghanistan, some of whom need everything from health care to housing. Regis immediately jumped aboard with me to do a benefit. He suggested we add Marty Short, who was remarkable. We raised a lot of money, and it all went to an organization that helps the veterans in every way—Help U.S.A. That's Regis. He's a one-of-a-kind package.

Maybe the best thing that Regis did for me was introduce me to Jack Paar. For you younger readers who possibly don't know, Jack Paar is considered the father of the talk show. I met Jack at a New Year's Day party Regis and Joy gave several years ago, and we immediately became friends. Regis and Joy, Jack and his wife, Miriam, who was as gracious a woman as I've ever met, and Elissa and I would regularly go out to dinner at a restaurant in Greenwich called Valbella. Management there would never let us get a check, but after a while we insisted. Of course, we then went there less frequently. That's a joke. Sometimes we would have dinner at Jack and Miriam's house, where I met several people who remain my friends today.

I recently was invited to a golf club to have dinner with some people Jack and Miriam had introduced me to. All the club members know each other. I got there early and went to the bar to have a drink. A woman seated there asked me who I was with. I told her, and she said, mentioning the hostess's name, "Oh, she wouldn't want you to be drinking *that*!" She asked the bartender to bring me something so upscale, even *I* could tell the difference.

Jack would hold forth at these dinners at his house where so many of us first met, and I loved it. Once there was a brief pause, and someone started to say something. Jack interrupted and said, "I'm forming my next thought."

At another dinner at Jack's, I was sitting next to Phyllis Diller, then in her eighties. I whispered into her ear, "I'd like to get you alone in a hotel room." She said, "I've had a hip replacement." I growled into her ear, "I don't care!"

About a year after all this, Jack saw a snake in his garage and fired a gun to scare it away. He later told me that snakes don't have ears, but the shot caused a hearing loss in Jack. He once wrote me a letter saying he felt I was going to ask him to appear on my cable show, which he would do only if Johnny Carson appeared. Of course, I had no intention of imposing on either one of them. Jack had said, "The way to remain a legend is not to appear." However, he chose to join me and Regis on my five-hundredth show. Regis credits Jack with his concept of host chat, a huge thing to all of Regis's fans.

Eventually, Jack's health began to fail. He had major surgery and someone left a sponge in him, which didn't help matters. Sometimes being a celebrity is a negative, because people get distracted. Not long after that he suffered a stroke, which took away his ability to speak. Jack—of all people.

I would regularly visit him at a rehabilitation center and often take Gene Wilder with me. Jack once said that introducing Gene to him was the best thing I had ever done for him. Gene would kiss him on the cheek and hold his hand while I did my latest riffs.

Jack couldn't speak, but he could smile, which he often did when Regis and I visited and tried to entertain him. When he passed away, I was given the honor of being the last speaker at the service. Earlier in the day I was on the phone with Ethel Kennedy, who was also a friend of Jack's. She said, "Jack's in heaven with Jack and Bobby." I asked her if I could quote her in my remarks and she said yes.

When my turn came, I told some humorous stories about

Jack and then finished by quoting Mrs. Kennedy. Afterward one of the other speakers, an atheist, said he really liked my speech, "Except for that last part." There's *always* a critic.

I miss Jack so much as well as Miriam, who is also gone. I doubt there will ever be anyone like him. Regis and I have never stopped talking about Jack and how much we loved him, and how much he did for us by loving us.

Paul Newman

I was fortunate enough to know Paul Newman. Years ago, Paul reached out to me to go with him and Christopher Plummer to testify on an issue at the state capital in Hartford. I agreed, even though I wasn't completely clear on what the issue was. I figured if Paul was bothered about something, it was at least worth my time to listen to him explain it on the drive to the capital. It turned out to be about protecting your movie image from being used at a certain point after you were deceased to promote a commercial product, without your or your survivors' permission. I was amazed that such a law wasn't already in place. I testified.

I later had contact with Paul when I was working on my book *If I Only Knew Then . . . learning from Our Mistakes*. Paul was the only contributor out of eighty-two people who said he hadn't learned *anything* from his mistakes, but he took comfort in knowing they were the same mistakes—not new ones. I can only assume I didn't know Paul well enough, because I never saw him make *any* mistakes.

I last saw him about a year and a half before he died, when he and his wife, Joanne Woodward, asked me to be a part of a fund-raiser for the Westport Country Playhouse. It was to be an evening of love poems. I consider reading poetry aloud not one of my callings—which is an understatement—but I agreed to do it, because it was Paul and Joanne who asked.

About an hour before we were to begin, Paul quietly asked me to remind him to blow his nose before we went on. When we were called to the stage, I said, "Paul, blow your nose." He did. Philip Seymour Hoffman observed all this, and I told him, "That's why they got me."

If it was a worthy cause, you didn't have to get Paul New-man, because he was already there.

Jack and Bob

My older brother, Jack, is extraordinary. Being more sensible than I, he became a CPA and an attorney. He has always been my biggest supporter. He knows I was elected president of my fifth-grade class, and then was impeached. At the age of seventy-nine he chose to tell me for the first time that *he* was elected president of his fourth-grade class. I asked, "Were you impeached?" He softly said, "No."

For someone whose father died at the age of fifty-two, I consider myself remarkably fortunate that my doctor, at this writing, anyway, has been unable to find anything physically wrong with me. He says, "I don't know what you're doing, but maybe we all should do it."

My brother, unfortunately, has been besieged by one illness after another. Jack has always been interested in singing. He has gone to retirement homes at Christmas to lead the people there in singing carols.

A couple of years ago, I sent him a big songbook that has most of the standards in it. I also send a keyboard player to his house a couple of times a week, so Jack can sing to accompaniment. He really enjoys that.

About eight years ago, I became friends with a man about my brother's age, Bob Ellis. Bob doesn't sing, but he is as goodwilled as any person I've ever met. Recently I gave Bob the same songbook that I'd sent my brother. And now Bob, who lives in New York, and Jack, who lives outside of Pittsburgh, take turns calling each other every day and singing about six songs together on the phone. In between they share anecdotes, and a great time is had by all.

I've produced in the movies, on Broadway and off-Broadway, and in television, but this by far is the most gratifying show I've ever produced.

Singing may not cure all ills, but it certainly moves us in the right direction. If someone in your family or your friends or maybe even you are down, it might be a good idea to get them singing to lift their spirits. I plan to do it myself.

Since I wrote the above, my friend Bob has passed away. I first met Bob Ellis when he came over to me after a benefit I did at the YMHA in New York City for the children of Bedford Hills Women's Correctional Facility in Bedford, New York. He introduced himself and said he'd like to produce a similar benefit in his area of Armonk, New York. He did.

Bob and I quickly became close friends. I soon learned he had multiple myeloma, an incurable blood disease.

Bob suggested we start a foundation. He wanted me to be the president, because he felt I knew of people in situations not widely known who needed a hand. We called the foundation Lend a Hand.

Through Jayne Begelson at the New York City Bar, I learned of two teen boys with cystic fibrosis. The average life span of people with cystic fibrosis is in the thirties, although some people have lived longer. Right now, there is no cure.

The boys were foster children of a couple in Pennsylvania with three children of their own. Bob arranged for the family, Jane Begelson, her sister, the family social worker, and her husband to join us on a fishing boat he chartered, since we learned one of the boys loved to fish.

We had a great time. Unfortunately Bob couldn't join us. He was in the hospital with pneumonia.

Later I arranged for the family to come to my house, and Bob came with one of his sons, a doctor. It was a magnificent day.

There was a famous band in the forties called the Tex Beneke Orchestra. Sometimes when I'd be hosting an event, I would introduce Bob—who was actually a semiretired real estate man—as Boppin Bob Ellis, formerly with the Tex Beneke Orchestra. Bob would stand up in the audience and wave. The audience applauded, and after the event some people would come over to him and ask if he still sang. Bob would say, "I hum a little."

I started to bring Bob onstage with me. Sometimes when I was talking I'd look at him as though I had no idea who he was or what he was doing there. He'd just look back at me with a pleasant expression.

In the fall of 2008, I hosted the annual Children's Cancer & Blood Foundation fund-raiser at the Plaza Hotel in New York City. Bob was to appear with me in a comic routine—no lines yet, but Bob would be playing the Plaza. He died five days before the event.

Since Bob would often join me at various events, he was at one where a photograph was taken of Eli Wallach, Jack Klugman, and me. I'm in the middle with my arms around Eli and Jack. Bob is on the side almost as if he's superimposed on the photograph, like Woody Allen in *Zelig*. I took the picture of Bob's face and had a card made that read "WANTED" on the top, Bob's face under it, and then the charges against him, "Seen taking funds from a church collection basket and crossing state lines for immoral purposes with a goat," and below that, "$$REWARD$$."

I blew it up to the size of an actual wanted poster, gave it to Bob, and hung another one in my study right where I look at a wall. It was always fun to see. After Bob died, it took on a new meaning because it read "WANTED" above Bob's face and was a constant reminder of how much I miss him. I had to take it down, because I don't believe it's helpful for me always to look at photos of beloved deceased friends, *particularly* if it says "WANTED" above their face.

I see people not as Republicans or Democrats, liberals or conservatives, but as those who care about others and those who don't. Bob Ellis cared. He was a wonderful role model, he loved to laugh, and he always seemed to be concerned about the other person, even if he didn't know you.

Can we still call people saints?

Elie Wiesel

I recently spent some time with the Nobel Peace Prize–winner Elie Wiesel. He is the foremost chronicler of the Holocaust, having been in the death camps as a teenager, where he lost his father, mother, and baby sister.

He vividly recounts his experience in his book *Night*. We made plans to meet again, so I felt obligated to read this book. I'm not lacking in imagination, and I've never felt the need to read books on the Holocaust, having come from an Orthodox Jewish family that had to flee Europe because of the persecution of the Jews.

The book was everything I expected, which means it put me in a kind of dark mood I rarely experience. It is hard to imagine that you could be taken from your home to be killed for no reason other than you were Jewish, but of course that's what happened as much of the world stood idly by. Reading the book forced me to confront something I've been avoiding my whole life, the role of President Roosevelt in all of this.

Here's what *Newsweek*'s senior editor Jonathan Alter had to say about that in his recent book about President Roosevelt, *The Defining Moment*:

FDR was not entirely negligent. In the face of an isolationist Congress and polls showing that more than 80 percent of the American public were opposed to easing immigration quotas, he raised the specter of the Nazi threat early, and sponsored international conferences on refugees. But Roosevelt did not bring the activist spirit of the Hundred Days to rescuing the Jews. It was never a priority. His 1944 War Refugee Board came years too late. And he made the mistake of listening to military advisors who said that bombing the rail and communication lines to the Nazi concentration camps in Hungary was impractical.

Jonathan Alter goes on to say: "Although bombing the camps themselves would have killed more prisoners, hitting the railheads—while unlikely to save many Jews—was worth a try."

The refugee ship *St. Louis* was turned away from the southern coast of the United States in 1939 under great congressional pressure. FDR thought that the refugees would be resettled in other countries, but most ended up dying in the Holocaust.

Eighty percent of the American public didn't want immigrants, even if they were going to be *killed*! I don't know how much of the public at that time grasped that reality, but the president and Congress?!

Are so many of us inhumane? What other conclusion can you draw? Most of us simply don't have any serious concern about others in the world who are being mistreated or even killed *today*! Is this a failure of human nature or of the media to better bring us face-to-face with what none of us want to look at?

Mark Twain said, "Moral Cowardice . . . is the commanding feature of the make-up of 9,999 men in the 10,000," and the experience of much of the world proves him right.

In accepting the Nobel Peace Prize, Elie Weisel said, "We must take sides. Neutrality helps the oppressor, never the victim. Silence encourages the tormentor, never the tormented. Sometimes we must interfere."

That remains true today. When you see inhumanity, speak out!

One of the many things I admire about President (formerly General) Eisenhower is that he made a significant effort to have as many GIs as possible see the corpses stacked like cords of wood in the concentration camps. It seems like it's just human nature that if something isn't right in front of us, we don't think about it. I try as hard as I can not to be that kind of person. I believe I have to try harder.

When my wife and I later had dinner with Elie Wiesel and his wife, Marion, I told him about our felony murder rule. I told him about a boy who was serving a life sentence with no chance of parole for a crime committed when he was home asleep in his bed, because he had lent his car to his roommate. Elie Wiesel, who has seen every kind of horror, stared at me for a moment, speechless. He then said, with astonishment, "In America?!"

My Family

For as long as I can remember I've been reading about people who resign from their positions in different professions and say, "I'm resigning because I want to spend more time with my family." In most cases none of that is true. They're not resigning. They're being fired and are given the courtesy to allow them to say they're resigning, and in most cases they really don't want to spend more time with their families.

My case is different. As I've said, I left the movies years ago because I really *did* want to spend more time with my family. My son had turned six and was going to enter first grade. I didn't think it would be the best idea for him to continue to travel with my wife and me all over the country.

Something had to give, so I resigned from the movies so I could spend more time with my family. I began my cable show in the New York area. I always loved to spend time with my family, but as years went by, my son got active in sports. My wife was getting book after book published. She was constantly being asked to write books. I've written a lot of books that have been published, but no one ever asked me to write one, so while I wanted to spend more time with my family, my family didn't really want to spend more time with me. Oh, they love me, but spend more time with me—I don't think so.

So the next time I hear some person who's resigning say he wants to spend more time with his family, someone should ask his family if they want to spend more time with him. Never assume *anything*.

My wife and son went on a trip recently. They, of course, invited me to join them, but they know me well enough to know I'd choose to stay home.

While they were away, I did something I'm not allowed to do when they're here, which is throw an empty water bottle across the room into a small wicker basket. Even then, I only did it in my study, not in the room in which I'm forbidden to do it. Their will is strong.

I thought I could get it in within ten tries. It took me fifteen. Naturally, I thought with practice I'd do better on the second try, but the second time it took me sixteen tries. The third time I was *sure* I could do it in ten tries, but it took me thirty-five throws to get it in.

I told this story to a friend of mine who was thinking of quitting her pursuit to be a nurse because of . . . something. She said that because of that story, which some would say was about failure but I would say was about perseverance, she decided to continue on her difficult journey to be a nurse.

By the way, when my wife and son got home, I tried it again in my study, and on my fourth try I went from thirty-five attempts to get the bottle in to twenty.

The lesson? Perseverance is a necessity whatever the goal.

A postscript. About six months later, I tried throwing the bottle in the basket again—in my study, of course. I got it in on the second try.

I like to listen to music on the radio, and maybe it's just me, but lately there seem to be more and more songs abut someone who can't go on without someone else: "When you came into my life, I knew you'd be my wife. Without you, I can't go on." "There'll never be another one like you. What am I going to do? I can't go on."

Now, it's nice to be with someone you can't go on without, but if you actually expect to feel that way most of the time, you have unrealistic expectations, which lead to broken relationships, divorces, and a lot of other bad stuff.

This is a lyric I heard in a song I was listening to recently: "If you'd stay, I'd subtract twenty years from my life. I'd fall down on my knees, kiss the ground that you walk on, if only I could hold you again." Now that's what you call being attracted to someone! Even more extreme is this lyric from *Kiss Me, Kate*: "So taunt me and hurt me, Deceive me, desert me, I'm yours till I die . . ." *Desert me*? I'm yours till I *die*?!

In the movies the young guy and the young girl are cute and charming even when things are tough between them. Try to compete with that in real life. In real life? The young guy and the young girl couldn't.

You're not always going to look up and see an adoring gaze from the other person. You're just not. You might even catch your partner in a "I can't believe I'm sitting here with this person" look. "I can't go on without you? You are my reason for living?" It's an interesting thought. Maybe we can all experience it from time to time, but personally I like this one: "Keep smiling. Keep shining. Knowing you can always count on me, for sure. That's what friends are for."

My wife saw me tell a story on the Johnny Carson show years ago and thought to herself, I'm going to marry him. She had gone to Dartmouth and had reviewed books and films for the *Times* of London. Elissa is an inveterate viewer of English mysteries. I'm just glad that before she met me, she hadn't met Alfred Hitchcock. She got an assignment from *American Film Magazine* to interview me and called. I accepted the invitation. She was totally professional and quite reserved, and yet one hour into the interview the tape recorder was shut off when I asked, "Who are you?" We discussed getting married within ninety minutes of meeting. I told my son about how his mother saw me tell a story on the *Tonight Show* and thought to herself, "I'm going to marry him." My son said, "She just didn't know you were never going to stop telling them." Since so many marriages don't last, we could all say making a marriage last may be the most daunting challenge. Any two people who spend a lot of time together will find endless things to disagree about.

In my experience most men feel women are too critical, and most women feel that men lack sensitivity. I'm sure some would say men are too critical, and women lack sensitivity. It's all true on any given day.

I heard one of my favorite comedy lines from the comedian Mal Z. Lawrence. A man gets up in the morning, crosses around the foot of the bed, his wife lifts her sleep mask and looks at him. The man says, "Good morning, dear, have I offended you in any way?"

However, in my personal experience, I know way more offensive men than women, but since I've never gotten out and around that much, who knows?

I do know this. The one essential ingredient a marriage must have is the knowledge you can *count* on the other person, no matter what. Other elements of a relationship may vary, but if you aren't sure you can count on your partner, and by that I also mean trust, your marriage most likely won't last. "Count on" to me means trust and goodwill always. I have that in my marriage, and I feel blessed. At this writing we've been married for twenty-five years.

Actually, I feel blessed in many ways. However, unfortunately or maybe in a larger sense fortunately, I am also on a daily basis agitated by knowing there are thousands of people among our 2.3 million prison population who absolutely should not be in prison at all! I've talked about them earlier in this book, but it's something I just can't drop. My intention is to make people as aware of this as I can, because when this fact becomes better known, this grave injustice and others could be made right. That's my biggest goal for the rest of my life.

The Diary

I recently came across a diary that I kept for one year in the early 1990s. For the most part, it expresses what I feel today. Here are some random excerpts, in the order in which they appeared.

- Extraordinarily rare sleepless night.
- Screw people who don't care about others.
- Startling how quickly I get bored. I was having a conversation with a perfectly good guy. It's me.
- Writing enormously gratifying.
- On work overload—watch out for compulsive.
- Going to try to slow down, not work nonstop.
- I'm going to keep doing what I'm doing—but at a slower tempo.
- It's all about effort.
- Saw Jeffrey Lyons at museum. He said, because I do many things, I seem like more than one person. I wonder if people resent that.
- Love Carol Burnett.

- Happy time with Carol Burnett.
- Nicky's birthday party wonderful. Elissa did a superb job.
- Great talk with Jack on phone. Absolutely no competitiveness. I'm so lucky to have him as a brother.
- Ran into Schwarzenegger. I asked him if he worked out. He wasn't amused.
- All in all it's a wonderful time.
- The filming is going well. Between doing the movie and writing the book, every free moment I'm really engaged which, of course, is the key.
- All is well. I'll take this kind of life anytime.
- Try to get company to be considerate of sick actors. SAG needs deputies.
- An excellent period.
- Some people don't get it. Respect, not aggression, is appropriate toward all.
- Life is excellent. It was a very good year.

What has changed as much as anything in my life is my former naively optimistic point of view. It's sad for me to finally realize how few people care about others, how many people don't mean what they say, and how many don't do what they say they will do: "When we say we're going to make your movie, that doesn't mean we're going to make your movie."

It's very important to me to do exactly what I say I'll do, and for people to know they can count on that. My favorite review came from what the editors of my high school yearbook wrote about me: "Chuck's a boy we all can trust. As class president he's a must." I've always tried to live up to that. It's a *way* better review than "If you want to know what it feels like to die sitting upright in your theater seat—go see this movie."

As far as how I spend my time now is concerned, the major difference in my life today is my involvement with prisoners' issues. My mind keeps going back to my grandfather sitting on my brother's bed all those years ago, telling me to better serve my father, because "his head is mmmm-mmm." That's the way my head feels today—for different reasons—but agitation is agitation. Still, as I've said, working on behalf of people in prison who shouldn't be there is the most gratifying thing I do. I consider myself one of the lucky ones to be given this opportunity to help.

Epilogue

So, I've been told in print in the early seventies, "It would be sad to think an acting career lay ahead."

Even though my cable show on CNBC was the highest-rated program in its time slot before or since, and the only show on the network to be nominated as best talk show every year there were awards, it was canceled.

On the other hand, once in the greenroom of a talk show I was spotted by Ringo Starr, whom I'd never met. He walked across the room and gave me a big, long hug. Neither of us spoke.

A silent hug from a Beatle can really bolster you, and that's what we all need to try to do for each other.

Acknowledgments

I want to thank my editor, Karen Murgolo, who is a most cheerful friend as well as a bright, gracious, and kind editor. I want to thank Karen's assistant, the up-and-coming Tom Hardej, for his excellent assistance. He, too, is extremely gracious and kind.

I want to acknowledge two people who have been in my life on a daily basis for several years: Jim Griffin and Rose Snyder, my agent and my assistant. They are excellent at their work, but most important, they are friends as well, which, of course, makes them the best kind of agent and assistant you can have. They are also gracious and kind.

About the Author

CHARLES GRODIN is a recipient of the William Kunstler Award for Racial Justice. He gained clemency for four women imprisoned under New York's Rockefeller Drug Laws and was cited by Governor George Pataki for helping get those laws changed. He is also the recipient of the HELP Hero Award for his humanitarian efforts on behalf of the homeless. He is best known for his starring film roles in *The Heartbreak Kid*, *Midnight Run*, the *Beethoven* films, and dozens of others. He has written six books, including the bestseller *It Would Be So Nice If You Weren't Here* and compiled *If I Only Knew Then . . . learning from Our Mistakes*. Mr. Grodin was a commentator for *60 Minutes II* and is currently a commentator for CBS News. He also writes a weekly column for the *New York Daily News* Web site.

One hundred percent of Mr. Grodin's proceeds from this book will be donated to Mentoring USA, where he has been a longtime board member. Mr. Grodin is also a mentor.